Taylor Wessing
PHOTO PORTRAIT PRIZE
25

NATIONAL PORTRAIT GALLERY

Contents

Director's Foreword

This year, the *Taylor Wessing Photo Portrait Prize* returns to showcase the works of leading contemporary photographers. From a total of 51 countries, we received 5,910 entries from 2,054 photographers; it is wonderful to see that submissions to the Prize are increasing year on year. The judging panel made a final selection of 54 works to be shown at the National Portrait Gallery from the fantastic variety of entries by both amateur and professional photographers.

In recent years we have encouraged artists to apply to the Prize through our discounted entry opportunities, emboldening artists from under-represented communities to participate. The increasing profile and thriving reputation of the Prize is testament to the brilliant display within the final selection. We are proud to be celebrating and spotlighting this, unifying people from different walks of life around the world. The final works were carefully selected by our great judging panel – my thanks go to Sunil Gupta, Katy Hessel, Sabina Jaskot-Gill and Tim Walker for their dedication and very valuable perspectives.

I would like to wish a warm congratulations to our prizewinners this year. First prize goes to Martina Holmberg for their honest portrait of *Mel* which brings strength to the portrayal of burn survivors. Second prize has been awarded to Luan Davide Gray, and third prize to Byron Mohammad Hamzah, both of whom capture intimacy in their exploration of overlooked communities. Every year, we select a Taylor Wessing Photographic Commission prizewinner who will go on to create a new work for the Gallery's Collection, which this year has been awarded to Hollie Fernando.

My thanks to the team at the National Portrait Gallery who work on the Prize year round; Grade Design for their work on the exhibition catalogue; White Wall Company for brilliantly managing the judging process; and of course to our longstanding partner Taylor Wessing for making the Prize possible through their generous support.

Victoria Siddall
Director, National Portrait Gallery, London

Sponsor's Foreword

Entering its eighteenth year, the *Taylor Wessing Photo Portrait Prize* has achieved new heights. The judges received an unprecedented volume of entries totalling close to 6,000 photographs submitted by over 2,000 photographers in 51 countries. The 20% increase in submissions from last year underlines the Prize's growth, alongside the National Portrait Gallery's successful efforts to broaden access to the competition.

We are delighted to be a longstanding partner of the Prize and to continue supporting the Taylor Wessing Photographic Commission into its third year. With two commissioned works already having been added to the Gallery's permanent Collection, we look forward to the third artist being afforded the opportunity to contribute to the world's largest collection of portraiture.

Many of the works in this year's final selection explore identity and community. The images provide insight into the lives of a diverse group of sitters; a diversity we are proud to support in our sponsorship of the Prize.

I hope you enjoy the 2025 exhibition and join Taylor Wessing in celebrating and congratulating the exceptional talent of the photographers on display.

Shane Gleghorn
Taylor Wessing Managing Partner

The Judges

Sunil Gupta
Photographer and Educator
Having followed the *Taylor Wessing Photo Portrait Prize* for years, it was a special and moving experience to be on the judging panel. Many of the images stayed with me long after I'd seen them – moments that spoke of tenderness, strength, and the complexity of human connection. Sitting with and reflecting on each image with the judges reminded me of the unique power of portrait photography to invite empathy, provoke thought, and hold space for stories that often go unseen.

Katy Hessel
Art Historian and Curator
It was an honour to judge this year's Prize alongside the other judges, all of whom provided a great lesson in what makes a 'great' photograph. I was stunned by the quality of this year's submissions and couldn't be prouder of our selection. From tenderness between lovers, friends and family to the raw truths of the world in 2025. Judging the Prize evoked the words of photographer Diane Arbus: 'I think there are things that nobody would see unless I photographed them.' It's this that we see in this year's exhibition.

Sabina Jaskot-Gill
Senior Curator, Photographs,
National Portrait Gallery
Reviewing such extraordinary prints with the judging panel in person encouraged discussion and debate – a democratic process which invited each of us to see the beauty of a detail that we might otherwise have missed. I'm so grateful for the time and care given by my fellow judges throughout this process, and to all the remarkable photographers who entered, whose work is testament to the creativity that abounds within contemporary photographic practice.

Tim Walker
Photographer
It was a privilege to be asked to be part of the judging panel for the 2025 Prize. Victoria, Sabina, Sunil, Katy and I as the judging panel came together, and we were all awed at the breadth and range of portraits submitted. In my opinion, the Prize is a mirroring of the zeitgeist and a portrait of the human experience, which for me is emotional and absolutely the truth; our chosen prizewinners reflect this sentiment.

Victoria Siddall
Director, National Portrait Gallery
and Chair of Panel
Reviewing such a strong selection of photographs alongside our very expert and committed judges highlighted the importance of collaboration – within their attentive and considered decision-making process, but also within picture making today. Works produced as a collaboration between the photographer and sitter gave us great insight into their identities and stories. The final selection of works reflect the breadth of talent in contemporary photography around the world that we are so pleased to showcase at the National Portrait Gallery.

The Prizes

First Prize

Martina Holmberg

Holmberg celebrates human resilience, empathetically depicting the strength of the sitter (p.8).

Second Prize

Luan Davide Gray

Exploring the journey of self-acceptance and representation, Gray captures an intimate moment (p.10).

Third Prize

Byron Mohammad Hamzah

In *Jaidi Playing*, Hamzah photographs a candid scene that brings humanity and calm to the topic of statelessness (p.12).

Taylor Wessing Photographic Commission

Hollie Fernando

Fernando's photography is enriched with deep folkloric symbolism to portray an all-female morris dancing side (p.14).

The *Taylor Wessing Photo Portrait Prize* is open to photographers from around the world, aged 18 or over. Exhibited annually at the National Portrait Gallery, London, the Prize showcases talented photographers, both professional and amateur. The winner of the competition receives £15,000, with second prize receiving £3,000 and third prize £2,000. In addition, the National Portrait Gallery awards an £8,000 Taylor Wessing Photographic Commission, which will see a photographer selected to create a work for the Gallery's Collection.

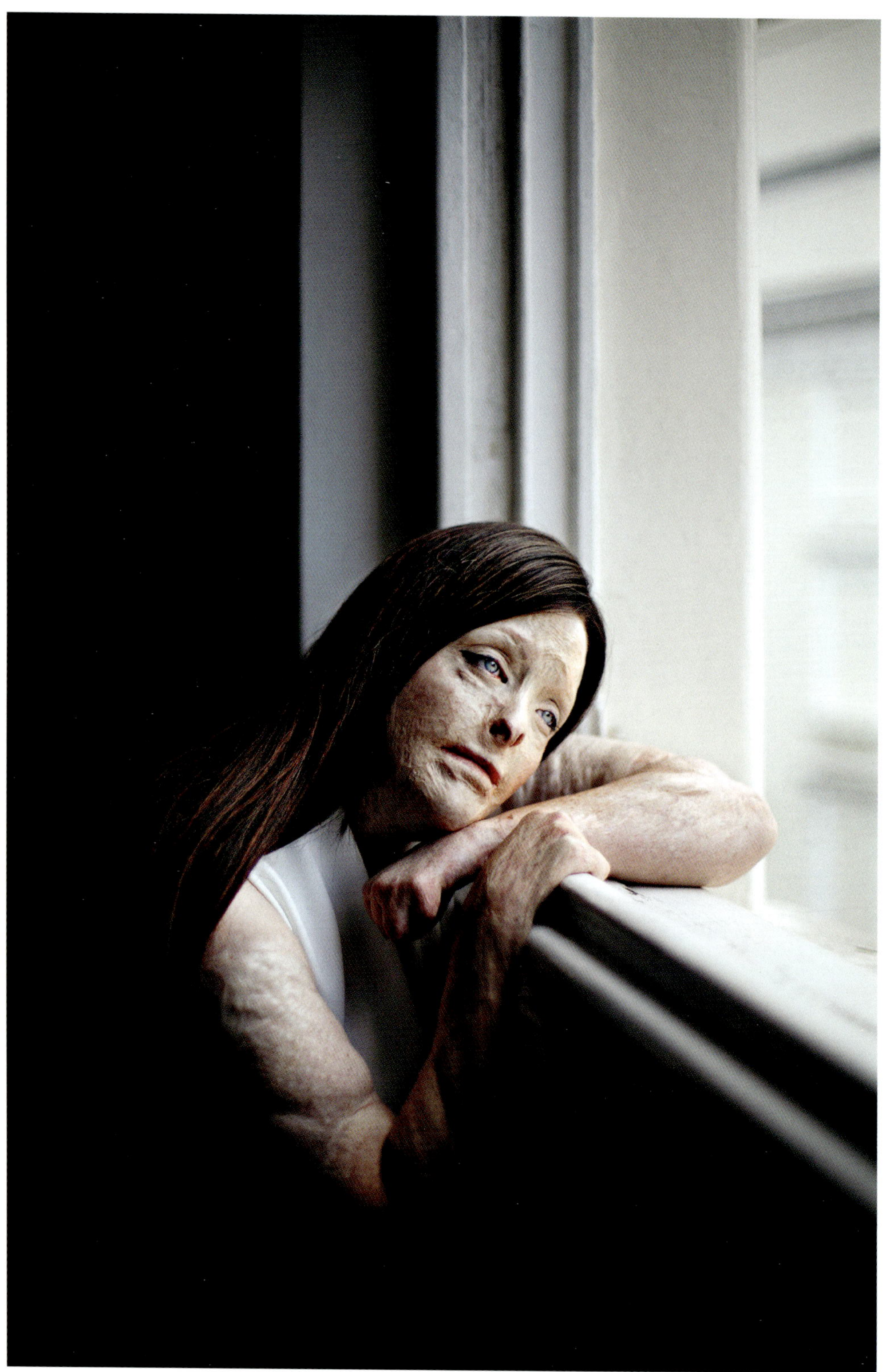

Martina Holmberg

Mel, 2024
From the series *On the Outside of Inside*
Chromogenic print

First Prize
Martina Holmberg

Martina Holmberg has spent ten years trying to find the 'right tone' to portrait making for her series *On the Outside of Inside*. Influenced and inspired by the series' sitters, the Stockholm-born and based photographer and writer explores diversity in appearance to expose discrimination while celebrating physical difference.

Her portrait of *Mel* is a collaboration, portraying strength through humanism and careful intention. The sitter's burn scars, while integral, are just one aspect of her life that this depiction makes palpable. Mel's thought-filled expression, her gentle resting pose and the way the cool London light from the window caresses her repaired skin, draws us close. It is deceptively simple, shot on a digital Canon, but the power lies in Holmberg's empathetic and refined approach; 'I want to take really strong photos of survivors not victims, to understand their trauma and feel their strength'.

Aged two, Mel was momentarily left in a car with her sister Amanda. When her mother returned from buying milk the vehicle was alight. Tragically her sister died, and Mel suffered severe burns. The cause of the fire remains a mystery, but Mel refuses to be defined through the physical suffering, PTSD and prejudice she has experienced throughout her life. Instead, she is a lawyer with a family, and an advocate for Changing Faces – the UK's leading charity concerned with physical difference.

Holmberg consulted Changing Faces, who helped her reach out to members to participate in the project. In return, the organisation can use the portraits in its campaigns. Here, Mel's hard-won self-acceptance therefore provokes further positive change. Words usually accompany Holmberg's portraits and will be part of the narrative when the series is exhibited at the Abecita Pop Art & Photo Museum, Sweden, in 2026, along with a short film – a medium she would like to explore further.

Holmberg's introduction to photography was through her father whose darkroom pursuits anticipated her career. Studying ethnology and anthropology grounded a deep care for and interest in the lives of others, particularly women, across the world. At age 26 she enrolled in The Nordic School of Photography – Sweden's leading school in photojournalistic storytelling – where she cultivated her belief in a person-centred approach involving discussion, rapport building and trust. 'It is not possible to take a good photo if I do not connect ... it is very important for me to try to understand – who is this person?' Searching beneath and beyond the surface, 'my aim is to make honest portraits.'

Holmberg's project celebrates human diversity. She challenges 'narrow ideals' by making visible the variety of 'what makes us human', promoting truthful representation in a culture obsessed with youthfulness and unrealistic visual 'perfection'.

Holmberg's practice is varied and her outputs generous. She has published eight books to date, ranging from *Fade to Black* (2012), which presents photographs made on joyously unpredictable and discontinued Polaroid film, to *In a Woman's World* (2021), in collaboration with journalist Maria Hagstroem, collating over a decade of global photojournalistic work with aid organisations. Holmberg understands the power of photography to therapize and memorialise. When her father became seriously ill, the series *Hanseman* (2016) became a declaration of her love and later loss. Today Holmberg is contemplating what to shoot on her father's unexposed film. She seeks a synergy between subject matter and photographic approach, alongside her deep-seated consideration of what it is to live in this world with others.

Interview by Clare Freestone

Second Prize
Luan Davide Gray

A loving kiss on a temple, a protective embrace, skin on skin. Luan Davide Gray's intimate portrayal of Mark and Giordano is a depiction usually absent from contemporary representations of attachment and relationships. In Gray's words 'their skin meets without barriers, telling a quiet story of trust, time, and love that defies convention.'

We Dare to Hug is a portrait of a couple in their early 60s. But beyond the frame it becomes a symbolic celebration of gay love, between two older men: 'tender and real'. For Gray it is the soul or essence of a person that leads him to make portraits. Mark and Giordano became collaborators with Gray after he reached out via Instagram. His own social media posts from several shoots with the couple have sparked his largest following, demonstrating the impact of this representation. For the sitters, whose personal journeys of acceptance are referenced in the title *We Dare to Hug*, being visualised by Gray and now exhibited has great power. The wider series' title is shared by the 2017 coming of age film *Call Me by Your Name*, celebrated within the LGBTQ+ community for its nuanced portrayal of a same-sex relationship and its exploration of universal themes of love and self-discovery. It is this universality and acceptance that is the essence of Gray's approach to portraiture.

During the COVID-19 lockdown, Gray, who had been working for 25 years as a hairdresser, evaluated his life. Crediting his Russian grandmother, a fine artist and teacher, for his creative sensibility, Gray was inspired to study Photography at University Centre Hastings, part of East Sussex College, validated by University of Brighton (graduating in 2021).

Gray, who likens his accent to a 'cocktail' due to his Russian, Romanian, Spanish and British heritage, was named Luan (with Irish and Albanian origins) by his grandmother. She named him after her friend who she had tried to protect from persecution for being homosexual. This story is particularly poignant, as when Gray's parents became aware that he was gay, they made him leave home. As a result, he was homeless for three years – an experience which has shaped his approach to human interactions and making portraits. 'I feel people in a different way' he says. Gray's interest lies not in everyday relations but in 'the real person, the sensitivity, the beauty.' In other projects, *Andrew and the Dog* (2022–25) and *Michelle – Hope for Tomorrow* (2024–25), he is greatly inspired by Don McCullin's powerful portrayal of homeless people in Spitalfields, London (1969–70). Gray's approach to homeless sitters is always respectful. He asks permission, pays for their participation and is honest about where the work is to be exhibited or published; but he would like to do more to help get people off the street.

Gray's mostly black and white portraits – he argues monochrome offers less 'distraction' – are often closely framed to an expression, or a moment of touch or embrace and quite frequently feature animals, for which Gray has an empathetic passion. Using both analogue and digital, his 100mm Canon and 150mm Mamiya vintage lenses soften poetic compositions and brooding faces captured in soft light. Gray's modest studio is currently in his London flat; it offers a controlled environment eliminating extraneous elements.

Gray's work continues to draw inspiration across media ranging from Lucian Freud's paintings of a sprawling Leigh Bowery, his own paintings reminiscent of Keith Vaughan and a growing collection of photographs including those by Brian Aris, Tony Kearns and Bruce Rae – a broad spectrum of representation with the essence of humanity at its core.

Interview by Clare Freestone

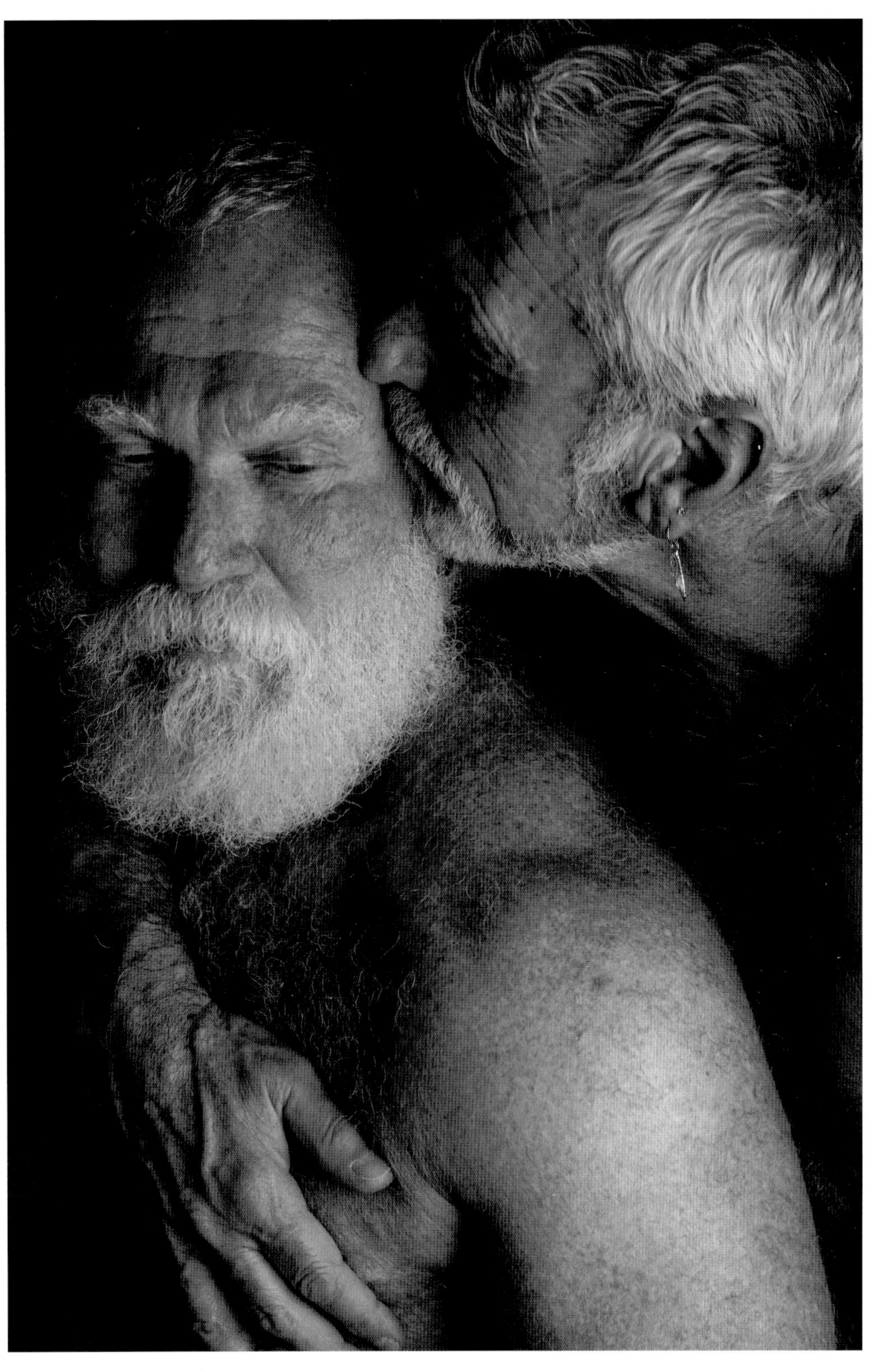

Luan Davide Gray

We Dare to Hug, 2025
From the series *Call Me by Your Name*
Inkjet print

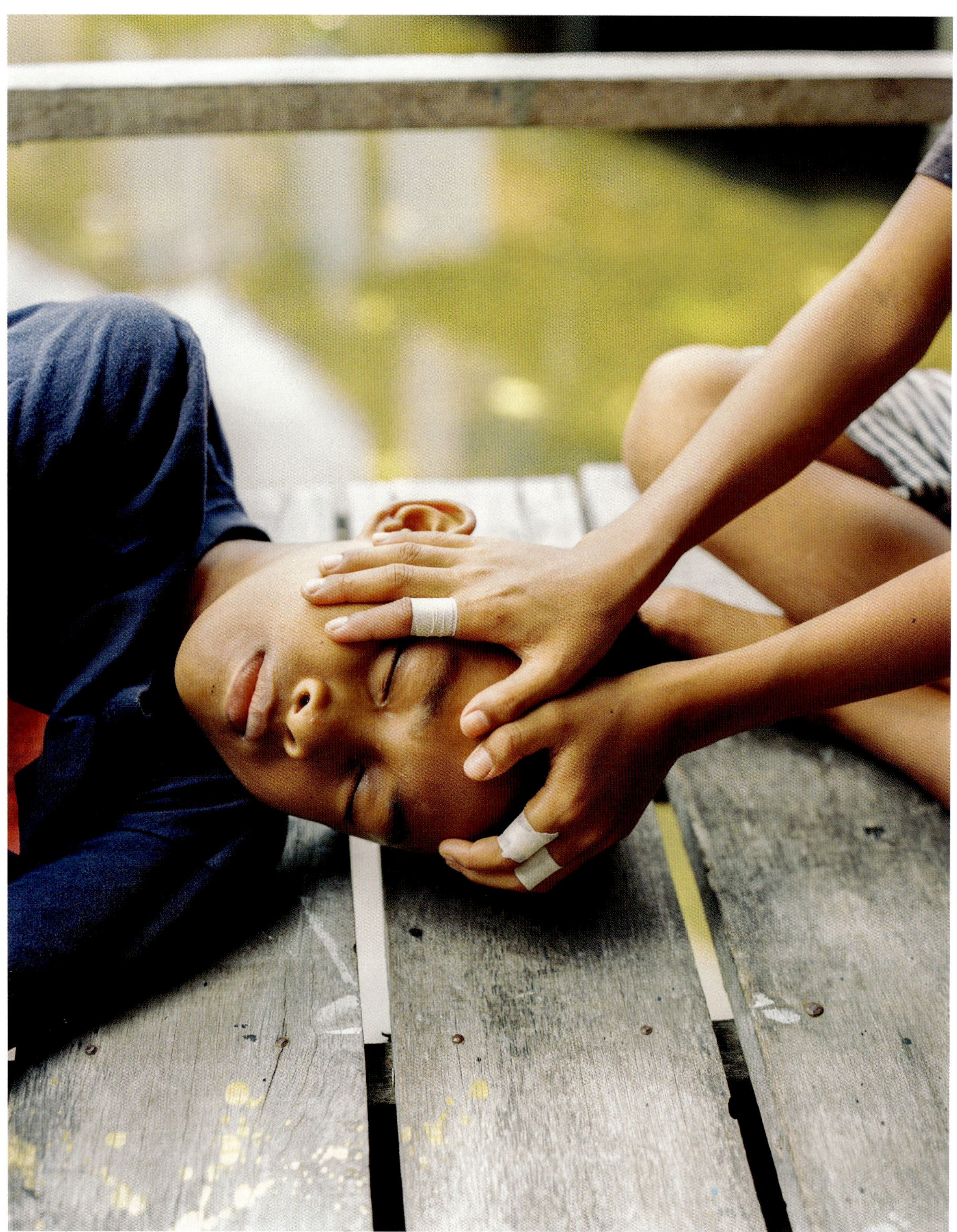

Byron Mohammad Hamzah
Jaidi Playing, 2025
From the series *Bunga dan Tembok (The Flower and the Wall: The Stateless Youths of Semporna)*
Inkjet print

Third Prize
Byron Mohammad Hamzah

Byron Mohammad Hamzah's passion for photography took root in his garden. The Malaysian-born, UK-based photographer bought a camera to share pictures of his flourishing flowerbeds with his family in Kuala Lumpur. His new hobby quickly bloomed, 'it took on a life of its own. It became an obsession'. YouTube tutorials gave way to a master's degree in Photojournalism and Documentary Photography at the University of Arts London, which he completed in 2025.

Remarkably, Hamzah has pursued photography alongside his day job as an NHS consultant. At first 'an outlet, a distraction to the realities of work', he now sees parallels between his creative and medical practice. Both require careful observation and a caring nature.

Statelessness is a complex and ongoing issue in Malaysia. Without government identity cards, countless numbers of 'invisible' people are denied access to basic rights such as healthcare and education. Seeking to understand how statelessness 'is affecting children at ground level', in 2023 Hamzah began volunteering with Borneo Komrad, an NGO providing free education to stateless youths in Samporna, east Malaysia. It was here that he met Jaidi, the 14-year-old boy pictured in his prizewinning portrait.

Jaidi's hometown of Samporna is populated by a large enclave of stateless people, particularly from the Bajau Laut ethnic group, a traditionally nomadic community who build their houses on stilts above the sea. For Hamzah, the contrast to his home city was startling; 'I thought I'd seen most of Malaysia, but when I went there for the first time it felt absolutely otherworldly'.

Living and teaching in Samporna over extended periods, Hamzah developed strong bonds with his students at the school. He noticed how Western photojournalism had portrayed the deprivation and hardship faced by stateless people in Samporna, but often overlooked the resilience, pride and determination of the community's young people. A more nuanced representation was needed; 'I wanted to show the hopeful side.'

Hamzah creates portraits of his students during their downtime outside of the classroom. *Jaidi Playing* reflects the relaxed informality of this approach. One blisteringly hot afternoon, Hamzah took his class to cool off on the sea-facing veranda at the back of the school. Tired from play fighting, Jaidi laid down to rest on the wooden slats, whilst friend Haikal began massaging his head, bandaged fingers gently framing Jaidi's face. With his Pentax 6x7 to hand, Hamzah recorded this tender interaction between two friends, unselfconscious in front of the camera. A moment of calm amidst a tumultuous existence.

As photographer and teacher, Hamzah is both an observer of and participant in life at the school. Inspired by the collaborative methodologies of photographers like Carolyn Drake and Nigel Poor, he encourages his students to annotate their portraits. Their comments range from hilarious to the heart breaking, giving voice to their experiences of statelessness whilst allowing their personalities to shine through.

Jaidi Playing forms part of a multifaceted and insightful body of work, developed over two years. The title for the project is drawn from a poem by Indonesian activist writer Widji Thukul, which Hamzah taught at the school. *Bunga dan Tembok, The Flower and the Wall*, contains a message of resilience and hope in the face of oppression – of seeds taking root against the odds. For Hamzah, it is a moving allegory for the experiences of his students. It also seems fitting for a photographer who found the power of image making through the flowers in his garden.

Interview by Ruby Rees-Sheridan

Taylor Wessing Photographic Commission
Hollie Fernando

A group of women huddle together, their flowing white dresses echoing the tones of the overcast sky. Flowers bloom across their faces and a beady eyed goat overlooks the scene. Hollie Fernando's otherworldly image of *Boss Morris*, the all-female morris dancing side, is brimming with folkloric symbolism, drawn from the London-born photographer's own journey into the traditions of the British countryside.

Enamoured with photography as a teenager, Fernando changed schools just so she could learn in a darkroom. 'I just absolutely fell in love with it. I lived in the darkroom; I'd eat my lunch in there.' Foregoing a university degree for a more hands-on education, she found a job at a portrait studio, 'working with kids and dogs and wrangling families together'. It was a formative experience, which the photographer credits for her 'amazing stress barrier'. Compared to the chaos of family portraiture, photographing stars such as Rami Malek, Rosamund Pike and Tom Hiddleston today is 'like water off a duck's back'. Her images are often infused with a dreamlike quality, incorporating rich colour palettes and natural elements, which lend her portraits a symbolic depth.

After relocating to Brighton in January 2020, the COVID-19 pandemic brought about a sudden change of pace. With the city locked down, Fernando began taking long walks in the Sussex Downs, and discovered the rich folkloric histories hidden within the rolling hills. The tales and traditions began to inform her photography.

It is said that currents of energy – known as ley lines – flow from Stonehenge down to Brighton, compelling people to settle in the seaside city. A stream of serendipitous connections also led Fernando to photograph Boss Morris. A regular photographer of the indie band Wet Leg, Fernando was watching their 2023 Brit Awards performance as the morris dancers joined the stage. Enthralled, she was moved to take their portraits. A mutual friend in Brighton put them in touch.

The prizewinning shot was taken during one of Boss Morris' practice sessions in Stroud, Gloucestershire, around the time of the summer solstice; the dancers' wildflower makeup and white dresses evoking the traditions of this ancient festival. Usually incorporating 'beast' costumes into their performances, Fernando captures a fiddle player veiled beneath a goat costume. This inventive, natural styling even formed the basis for a modern folktale: Boss Morris dancer Rhia Davenport penned *The Mossy Babber*. After setting up the shot, Fernando paused, waiting for the group to shift out of their poses before closing the shutter. The result is an intriguing exchange of glances that draws us into the frame.

The title of the resulting series, *Hoydenish* – meaning a boisterous woman – celebrates Boss Morris' disruptive and progressive approach. 'They are doing an age-old tradition of morris dancing,' Fernando explains. 'But they are not reenacting, they are reinventing'. She regards the group as part of a wider British folk revival amongst younger generations that emerged during the pandemic, and that despite 'everything that's going wrong in the world, young people are looking for connection and going back to their roots, back to age-old traditions.'

Winning the Commission has compelled Fernando to look back on her own creative roots. It is a poignant moment, not only because she has attended the Prize's annual exhibition since the age of 15, but also because this year's selection panel included her favourite photographer, Tim Walker. It is a testament to her talent and commitment as an image maker, compelled by the currents of her own photographic ley lines.

Interview by Ruby Rees-Sheridan

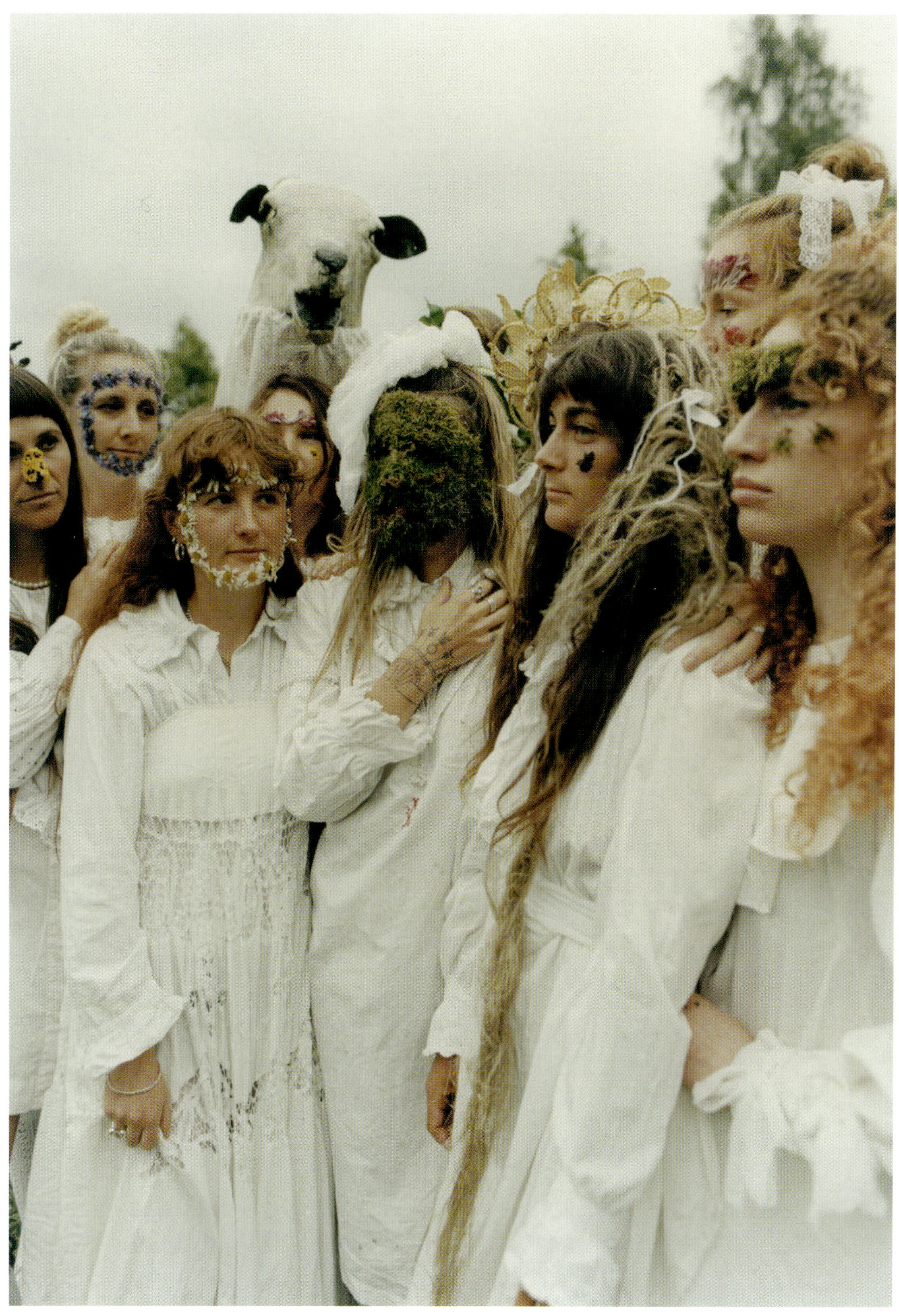

Hollie Fernando

Boss Morris, 2024
From the series *Hoydenish*
Chromogenic print

Exhibitors

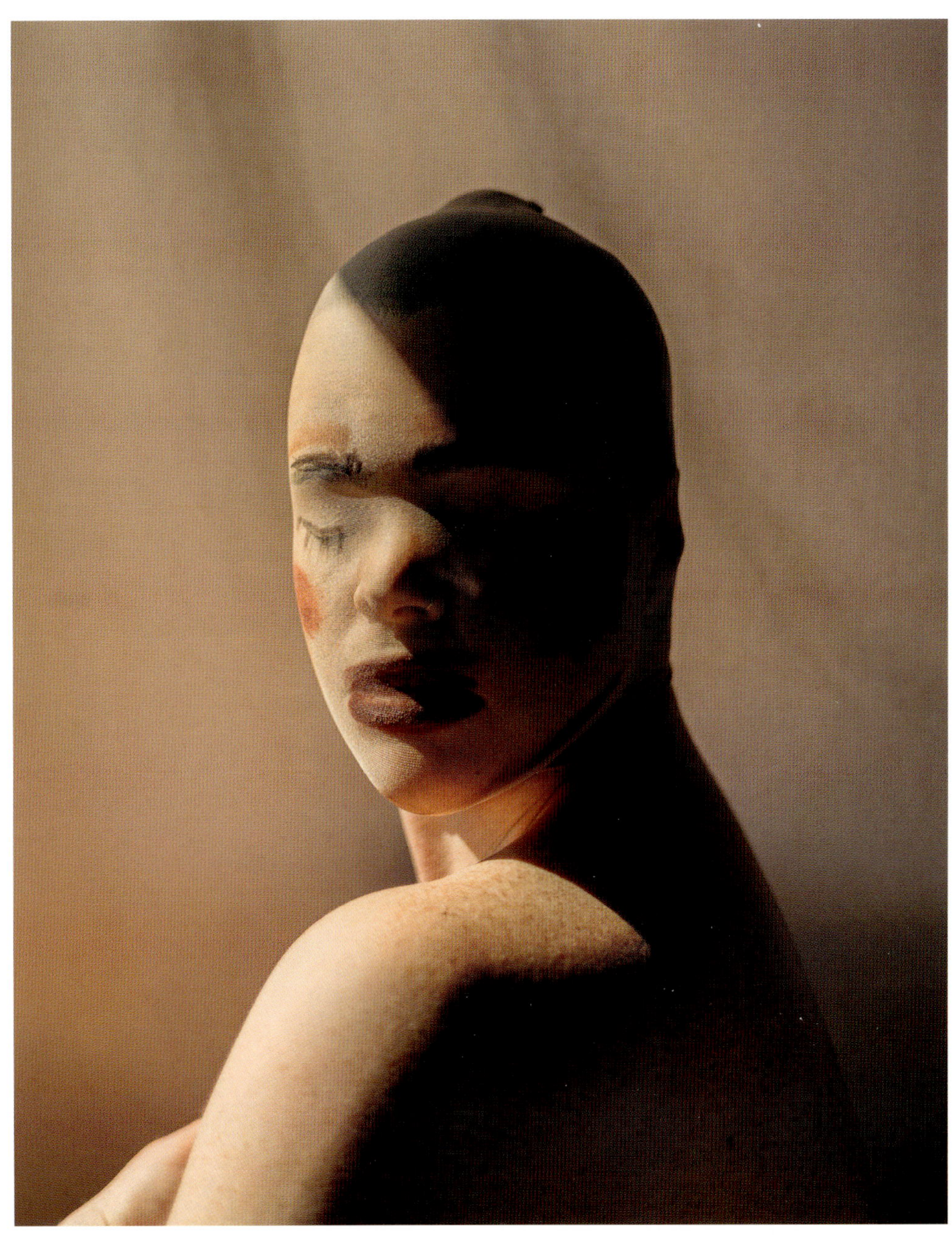

Charli Baker
Masked Warrior, 2025
From the series *Warrior Woman*
Inkjet print

This self-portrait by British photographer Charli Baker plays with ideas of entrapment, disguise, and distortion. With eyes closed, she seems to resist the bright natural sunlight falling diagonally across her face. The nylon stocking pulled over Baker's head combined with her exaggerated make up suggests a moment of surreal performance. The viewer is forced to question the sitter's identity, conveying a sense of imminent transformation in the light, pose and expression. As Baker writes: 'Perhaps I was a warrior in a previous life'.

Mahtab Hussain

Imtiaz, 2024
From the series *What Did You Want To See?*
Inkjet print

Social commentary artist Mahtab Hussain asked himself 'if this were the only portrait to remember my mum by, what would it show?' Imtiaz's gaze is unwavering as she stands defiant in her richly patterned kurta. The portrait formed part of Hussain's Ikon Gallery exhibition *What Did You Want to See?* (2025) which explored the richness and resilience of Birmingham's Muslim communities. Proud and monumental portraits, including this one of his mother, celebrate individuality and counter stereotypical representations.

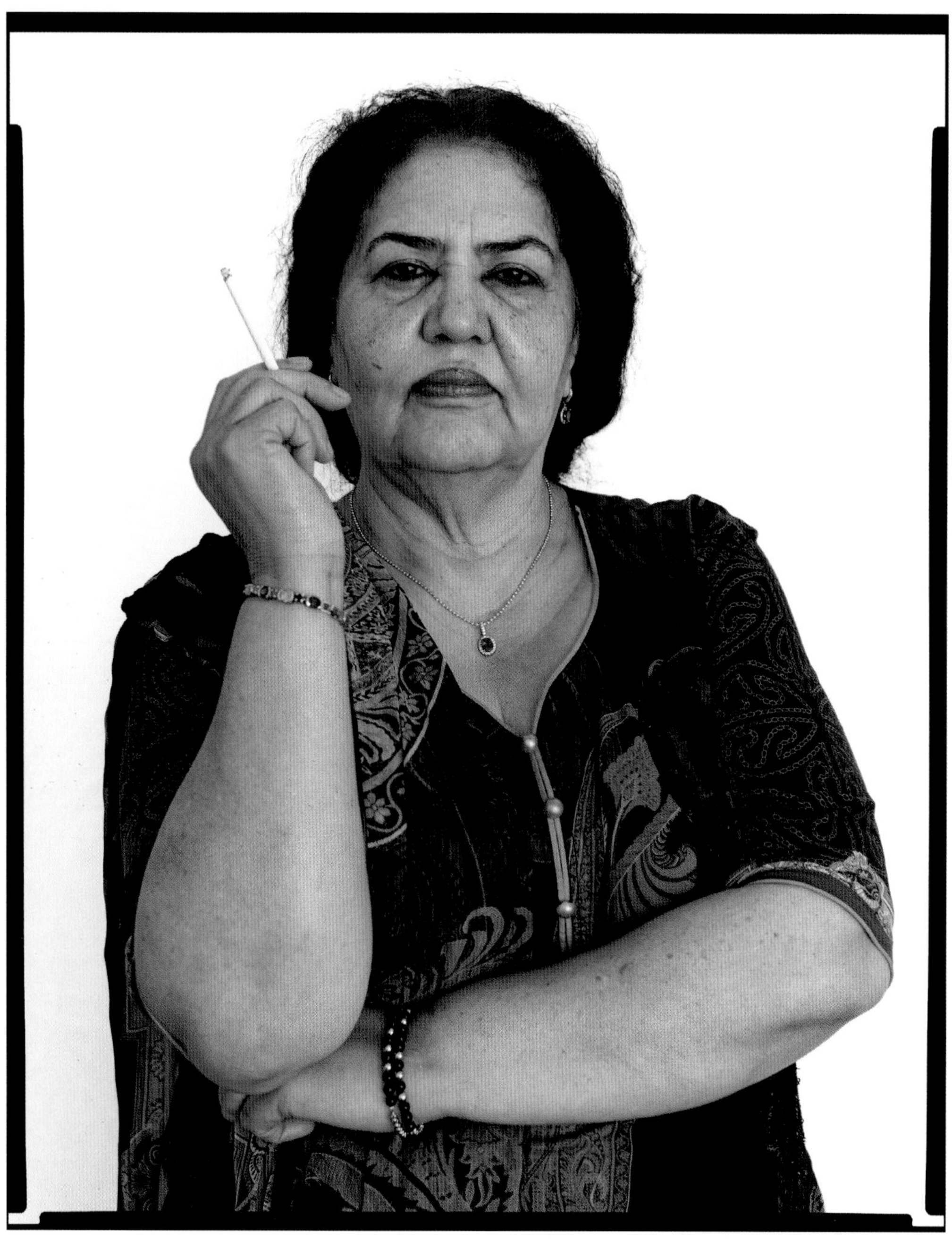

Roj Whitelock
Phil, 2025
Chromogenic print

The joyful rhyming of the colour pink in this witty image contrasts starkly with the sitter's grave expression and the unrelenting stare of his rich blue eyes. British photographer Roj Whitelock's portrait of his friend Phil provides a narrative through objects, pose and colour. Whitelock focuses on the sitter's extroverted personality in contrast to their experience of periods of isolation and introspection. The yarn relates to Phil's love of knitting while also symbolising something more indefinite about the 'unravelling of the self'.

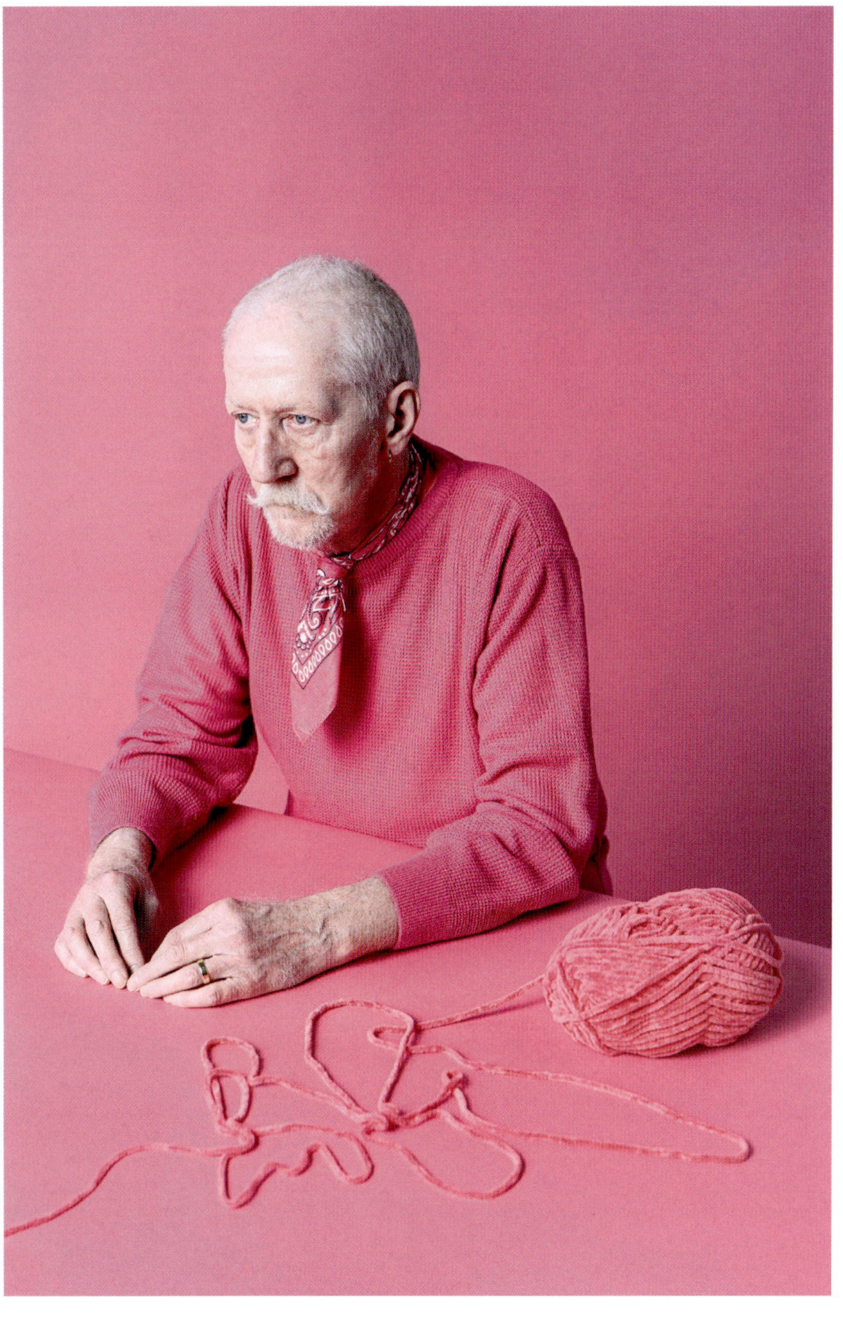

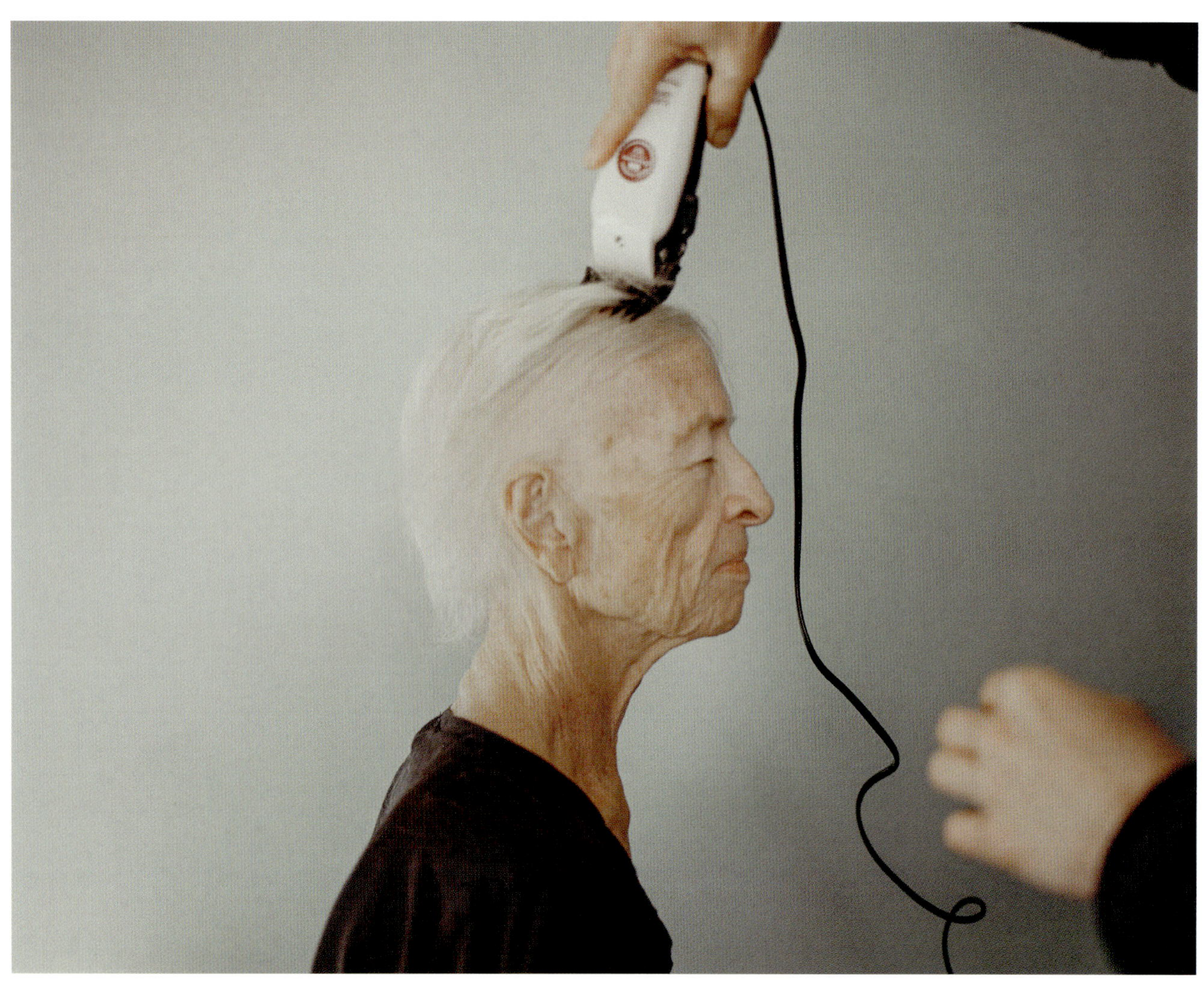

Joel Redman
Mum and Gem, 2024
From the series *Before Time Leaves Its Fleeting Trace*
Inkjet print

British artist Joel Redman deviates from his international focus on communities and landscapes to capture an intimate portrait of his mother who is living with cancer and undergoing chemotherapy. The photographer's partner Gemma frames the image, shaver in hand. Documenting his mother's decision to shave her hair, Redman marks the loss of her familiar appearance while embracing her evolving identity post-diagnosis.

Marc Sethi

Miles, 2025
From the series *Mencap Across the Country*
Inkjet print

Sitting on the edge of his bed, looking down the lens of British photographer Marc Sethi's camera, is Miles. Extremely active, sociable and with a 'cheeky sense of humour', Miles is surrounded by his collection of soft toys, mostly monkeys. This portrait was part of a commission for Mencap, a charity which supports people with learning disabilities across the UK. The project aims to document the stories and express the humanity of those living with a learning disability, along with their families and carers.

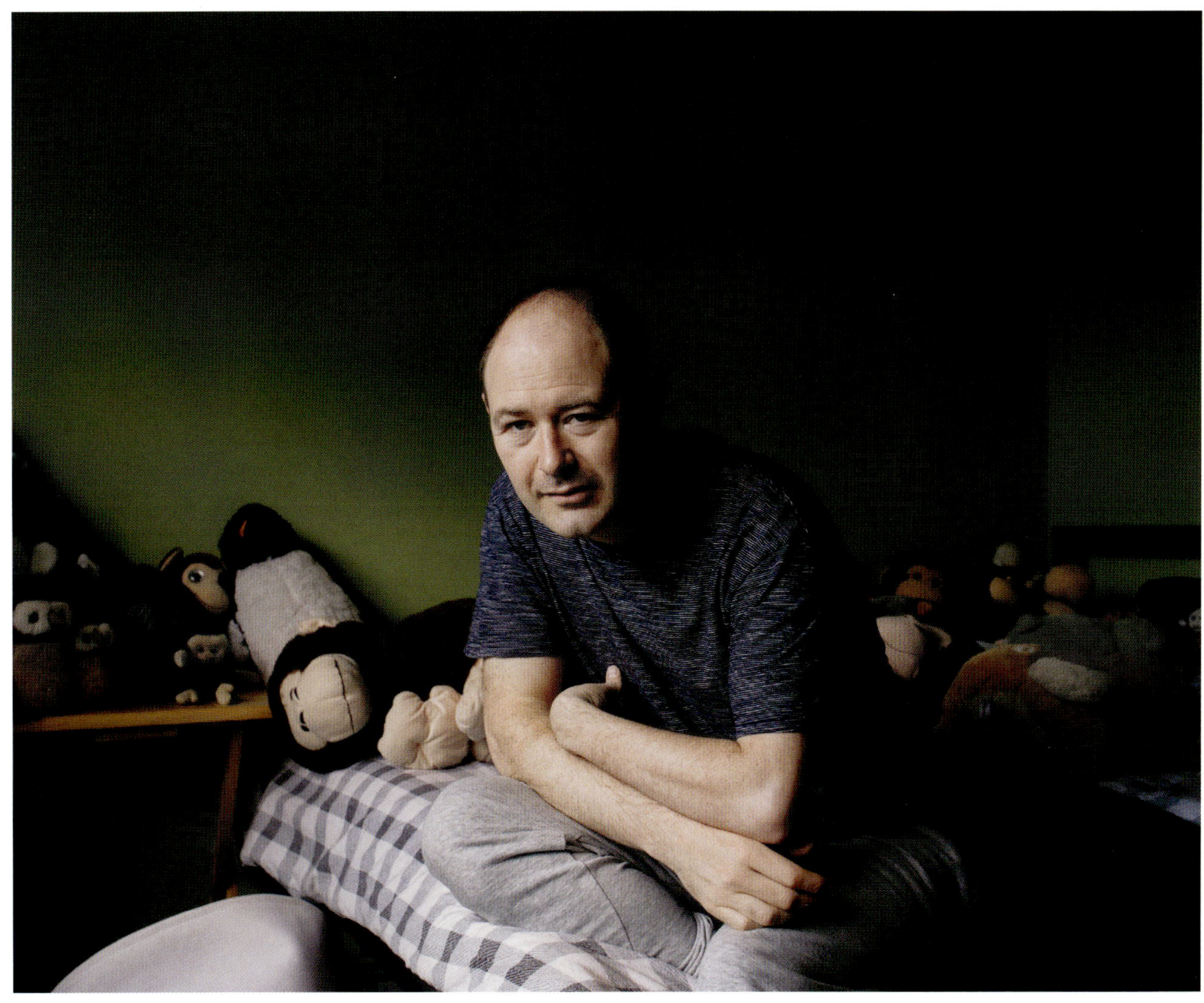

Catherine Hyland

Real Love, 2024
Destination Culture, 2024
From the series *New World Other*
Inkjet prints

Nestled in the valleys of Southwestern China, the ancient town of Dali is on the brink of major change. Young communities have settled there to escape the relentless work cycles, high living costs and repressive environment of the country's megacities. Catherine Hyland explores the role of photography in this 'back-to-the-land' trend. This surreal scene shows couples in white dresses and tuxedos scattered across a dramatic landscape in the nearby Yulong Snow Mountains. They are having their portraits taken as part of the booming pre-wedding photoshoot industry, a communal act of picture making that reveals how both humanity and the land are changing economically and in the cultural imaginary.

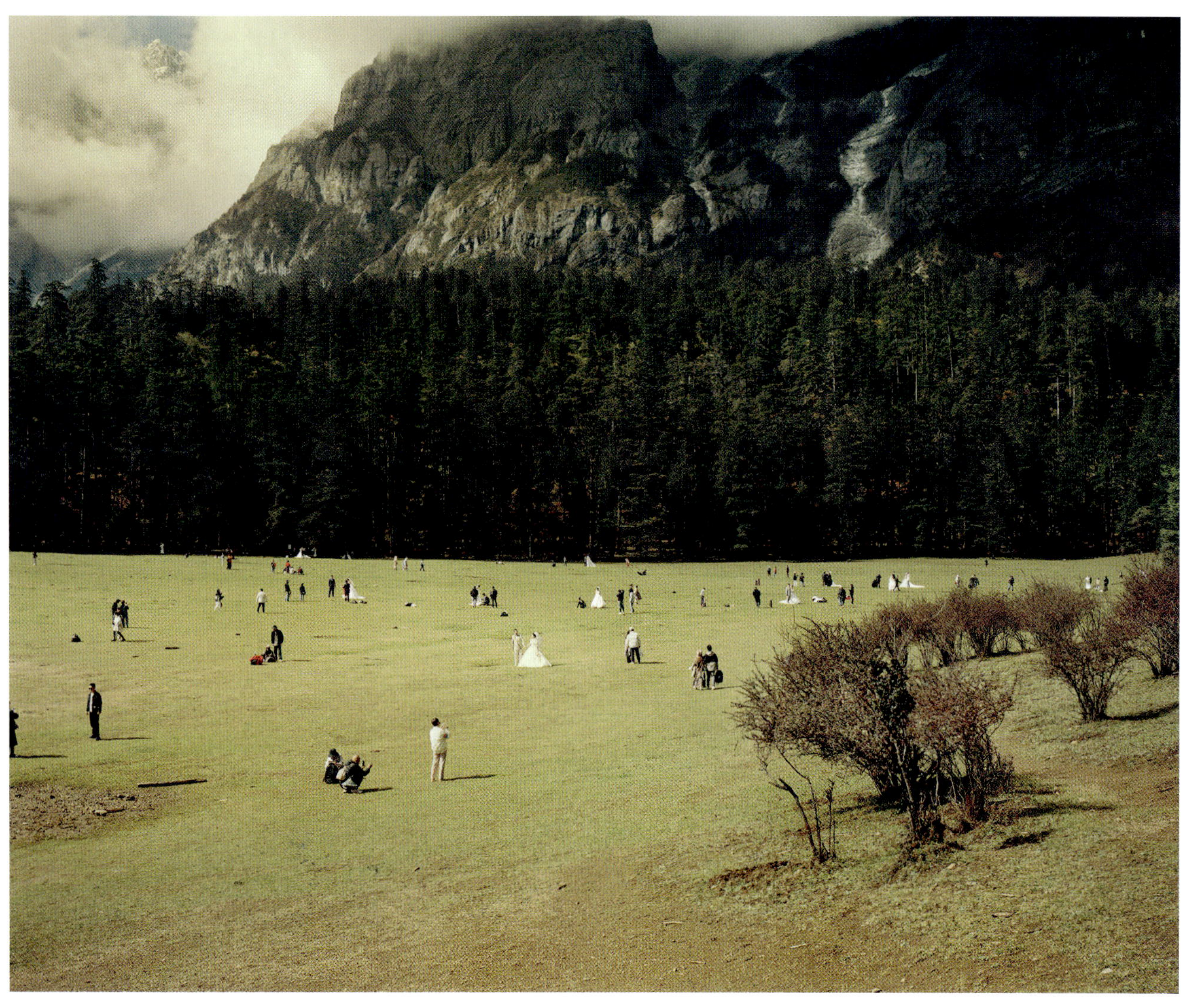

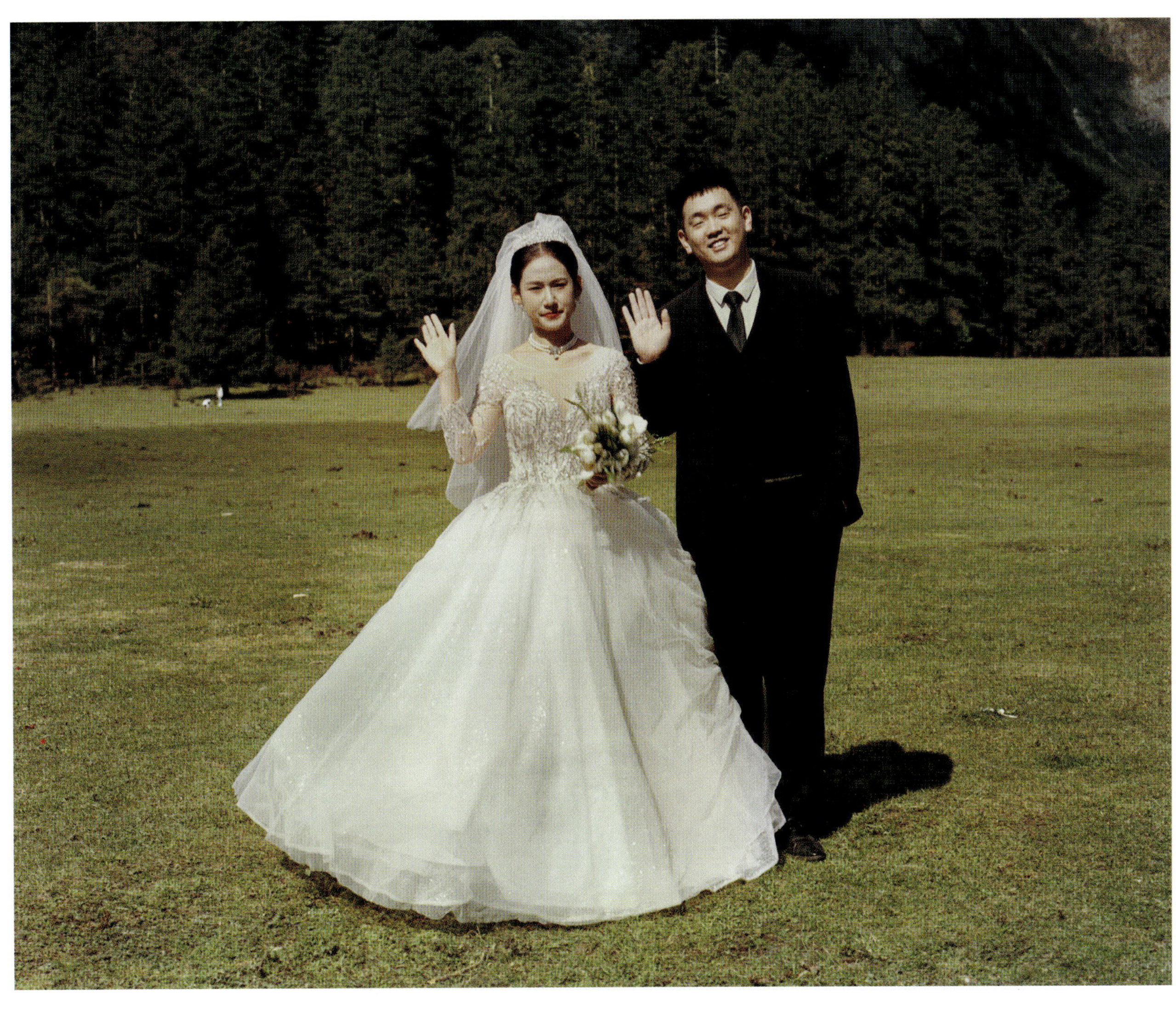

Betty Oxlade-Martin
Masked Pierrot, 2025
From the series *The Shape of Belonging*
Chromogenic print

In the midst of the procession of the Carnaval de
Binche in Belgium we see a group of school children,
all dressed in the costume of Pierrot, a sad pantomime
clown. London-based photographer Betty Oxlade-Martin
explains that the central figure, slightly taller than her
companions, caught her attention. Although the costume
is playful, 'something about her presence made it feel
more serious'. The portrait interrogates ideas of display
and concealment, history and tradition, producing a
beguiling image of contemporary cultural performance
and collective celebration.

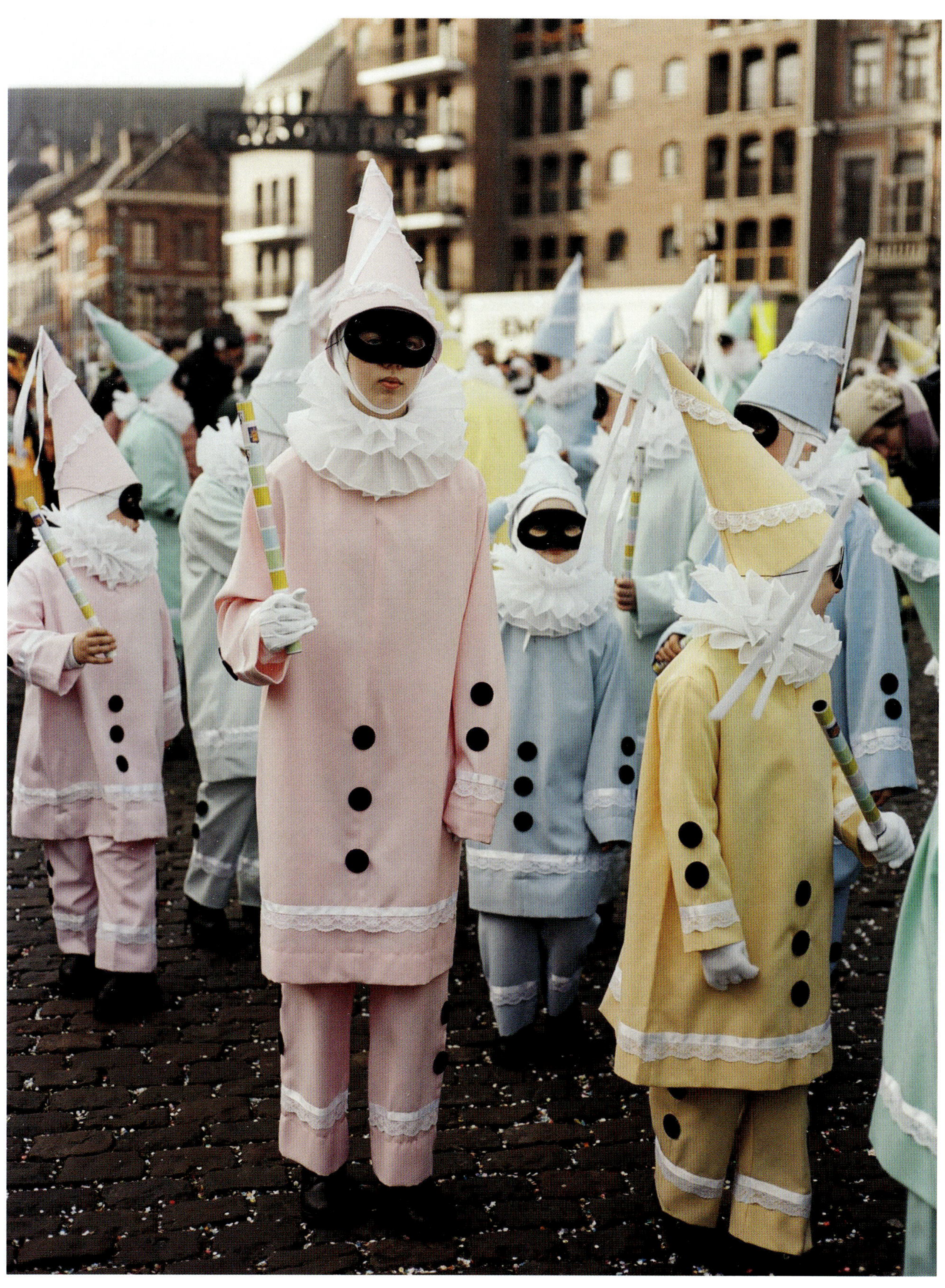

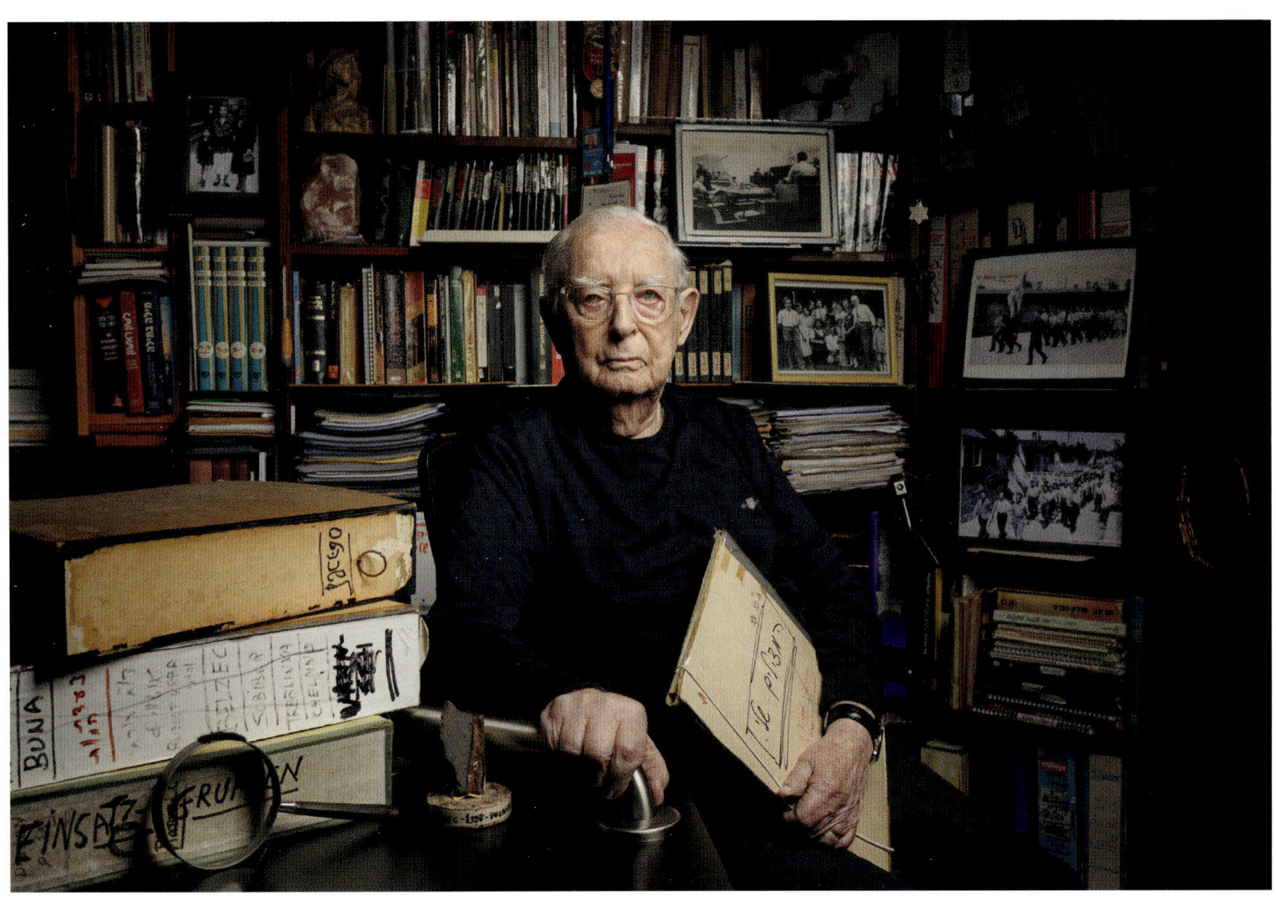

Jonathan Bloom
Michael Goldman-Gilad, 2025
Chromogenic print

Michael Goldman-Gilad, a holocaust survivor, is depicted with his hand gripping a rail as if to ground him amid the array of memories visualised through papers, books and photographs in his home. The file he holds is inscribed 'my saviours' in Hebrew, while others relate to his role as a principal investigator in the trial of Nazi war criminal Adolf Eichmann. Bloom photographed 'Miki', as he is known, following the release of his book *80 Lashes and One More*. The title refers to Miki's personal experience during the holocaust, the 81st lash relating to the many who 'disbelieved our accounts of the atrocities' following the war.

Lou Jasmine

To Know You, Still, 2024
From the series *Hold Me Here*
Chromogenic print

For a short period, London-based photographer Lou Jasmine stopped photographing her grandmother because watching her suffer with dementia was too painful. But eventually, photography helped Jasmine 'reconnect and stop searching for who she used to be but start seeing who she still was'. Composed with a tenderness, *To Know You, Still* confronts feelings of impending loss. Jasmine's portrait accepts her grandmother's vulnerability but honours her identity. 'This is a love letter to my Granny', she says. 'To strength. To history. To her'.

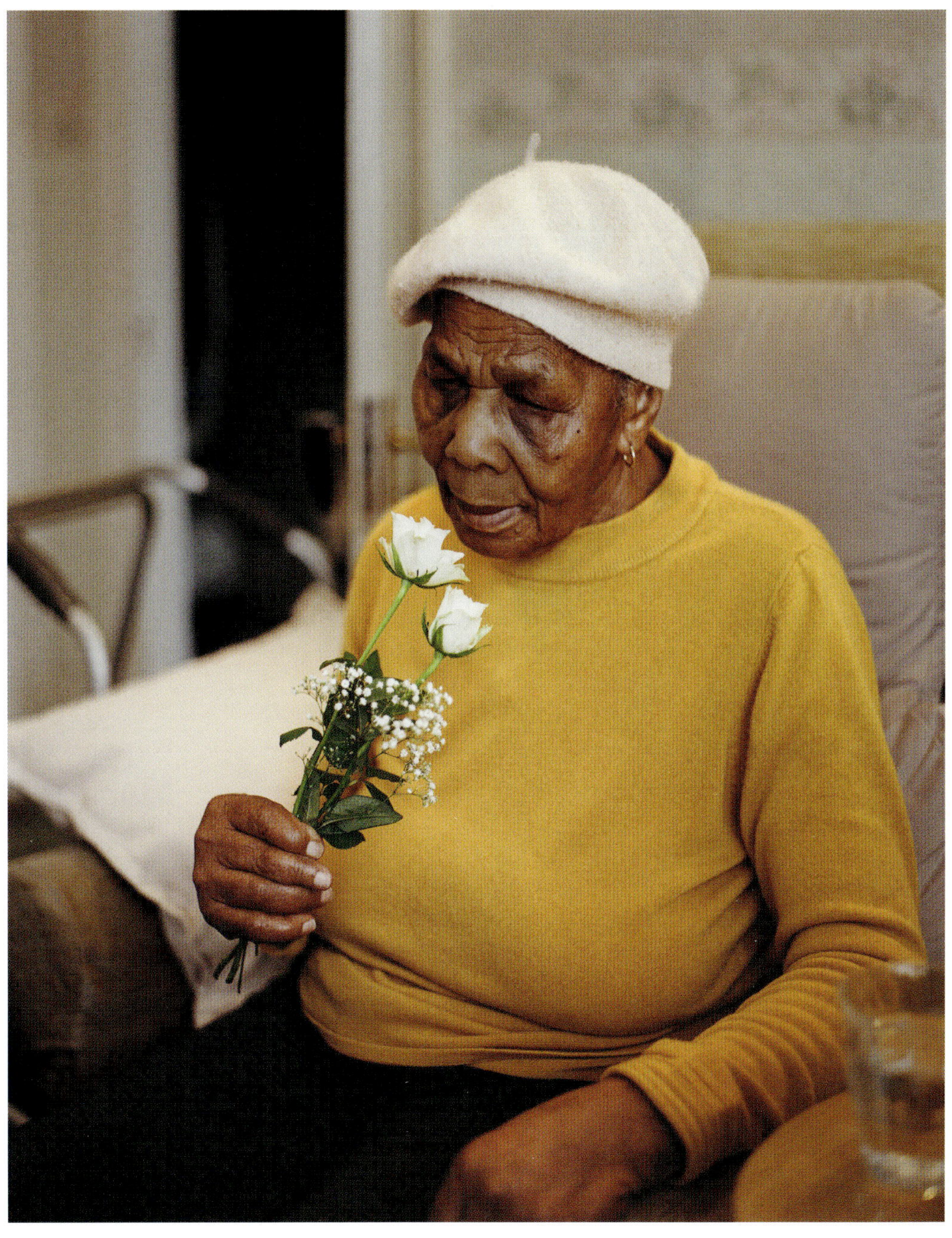

Mark Lamb

Precious Things in the Stream of Time, 2024
Inkjet print

Mark Lamb's portrait of his wife Enid slowly unveils layers of meaning. The undulating patterns forming in the background repeat the flowing hair of both Enid and her dog, their closeness speaking to their tender relationship. At the same time, the profound emotions present in Enid's staring eyes, together with the closeness of the composition, which details the textures of her skin, evoke themes of flux, transience and loss. British photographer Lamb explains that this portrait, *Precious Things in the Stream of Time*, allows him to 'preserve that which I hold dear, and which will not be with me forever.'

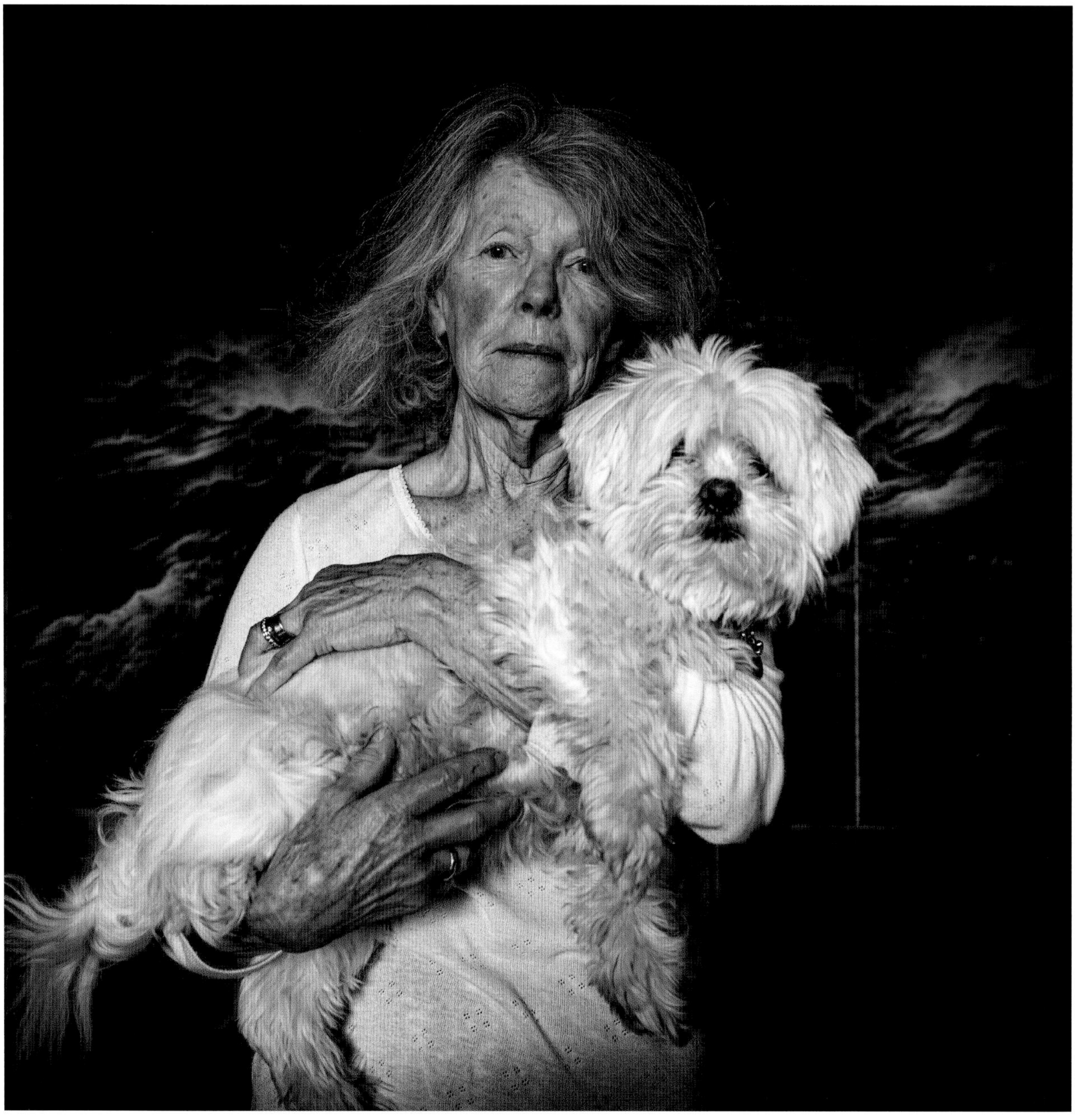

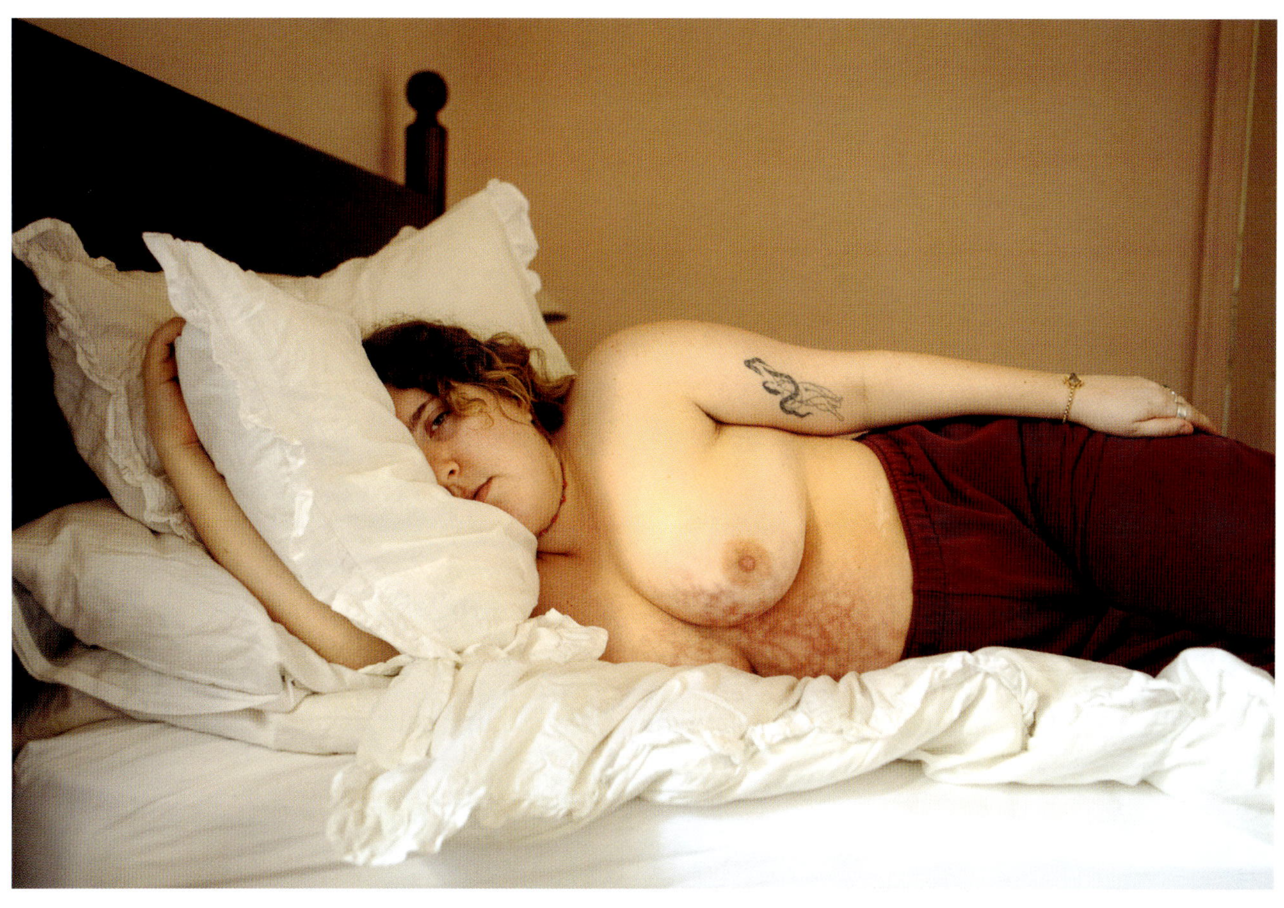

Margaux Revol

In the Agony Hole, 2025
From the series *The Pain Fugue*
Inkjet print

In this depiction of physical suffering, Margaux Revol pictures her friend Augustine looking beyond the viewer. Her senses dulled with chronic pain caused by endometriosis, she calls this her 'agony hole'. We are drawn to raging marbled red burn marks on her torso, caused by overuse of a hot water bottle in an attempt to ease the pain. The camera's intimate angle invites us to empathise with Augustine; amid the soft furnishings of her bedroom, we witness an endurance that due to lack of awareness and stigma is often silent.

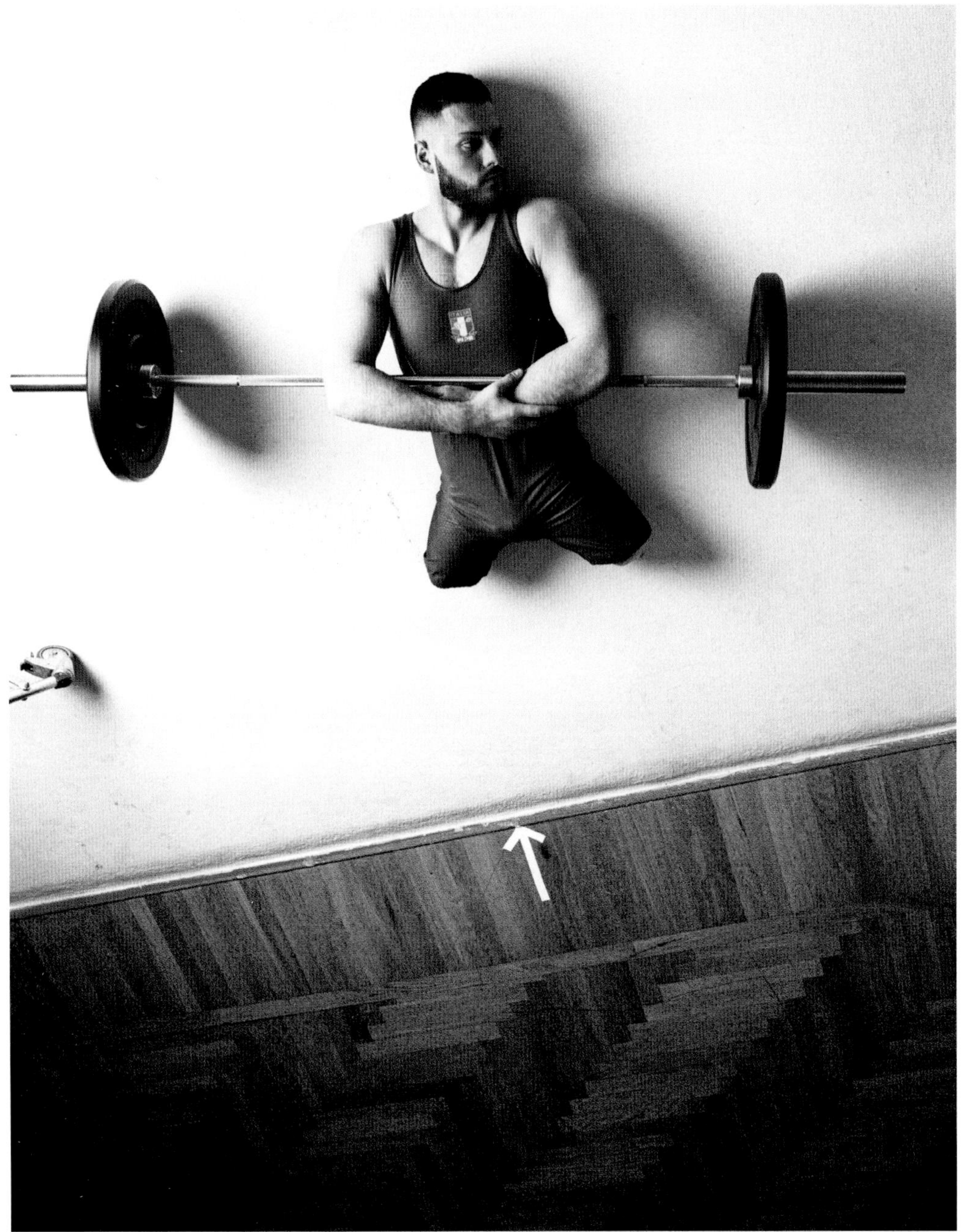

Mattia Zoppellaro
Donato Telesca, 2024
From the series *Physique Du Rôle*
Inkjet print

Based in London and Milan, photographer Mattia Zoppellaro's portrait of Italian powerlifter Donato Telesca is spatially disorientating yet deeply moving. The image was taken in the run up to the Paris Paralympic Games in 2024, where Telasca won a bronze medal. Shot from above, the photograph incorporates 'deliberately imperfect' elements in the composition – the metal wheel and the taped arrow. The portrait presents an image of order and strength, confounding and reconfiguring the viewer's expectation of disability.

Tom Parker

Contortionism Ulaanbaatar, 2024
From the series *Mongolia Modern*
Inkjet print

With their triangulated legs framing the vast Mongolian grasslands behind them, student contortionists Norovbadam, Misheel and Anungoo perform a complex manoeuvre. Contortionism is a national art form in Mongolia, with intensive training beginning at a young age. British photographer Tom Parker arranged this shoot as part of a broader series documenting modern Mongolia. Here, he captures an important aspect of their culture within a significant part of the country's 'physical and mental landscape'.

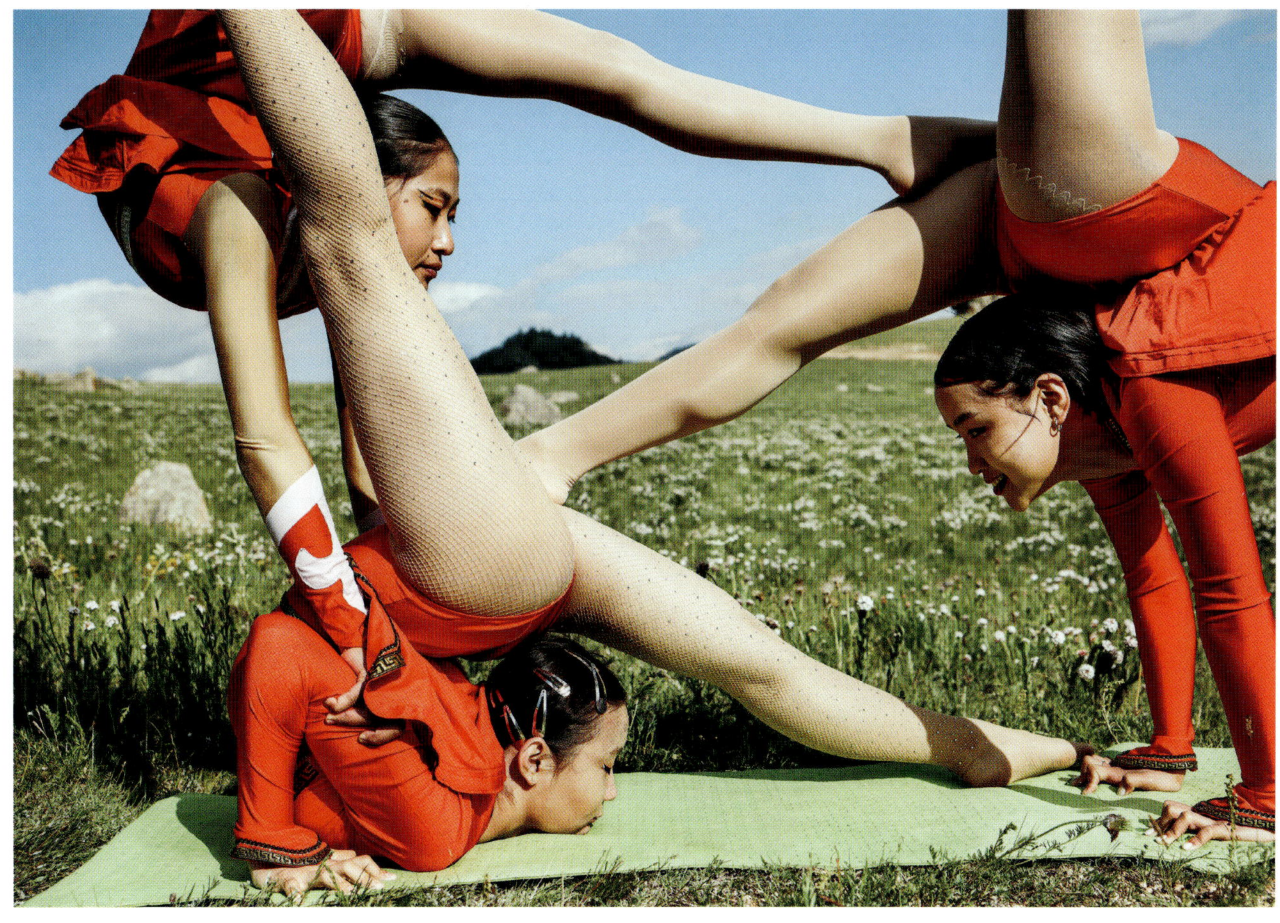

Chan-yang Kim

Backstage, 2024
From the series *DONGPO*
Inkjet print

In this vivid portrait by British-Korean photographer Chan-yang Kim, two cultures meet within the frame. Dressed in vibrant Korean hanbok, Jung-sook and Soon-hee were preparing to perform a traditional fan dance when the two young dancers behind passed by. The girls' red-crossed Union Jack flags and bright blue tutus echo the shades of the tied ribbons and embroidered flowers decorating Jung-sook and Soon-hee's hanboks, creating a harmonious image of cultural contrasts.

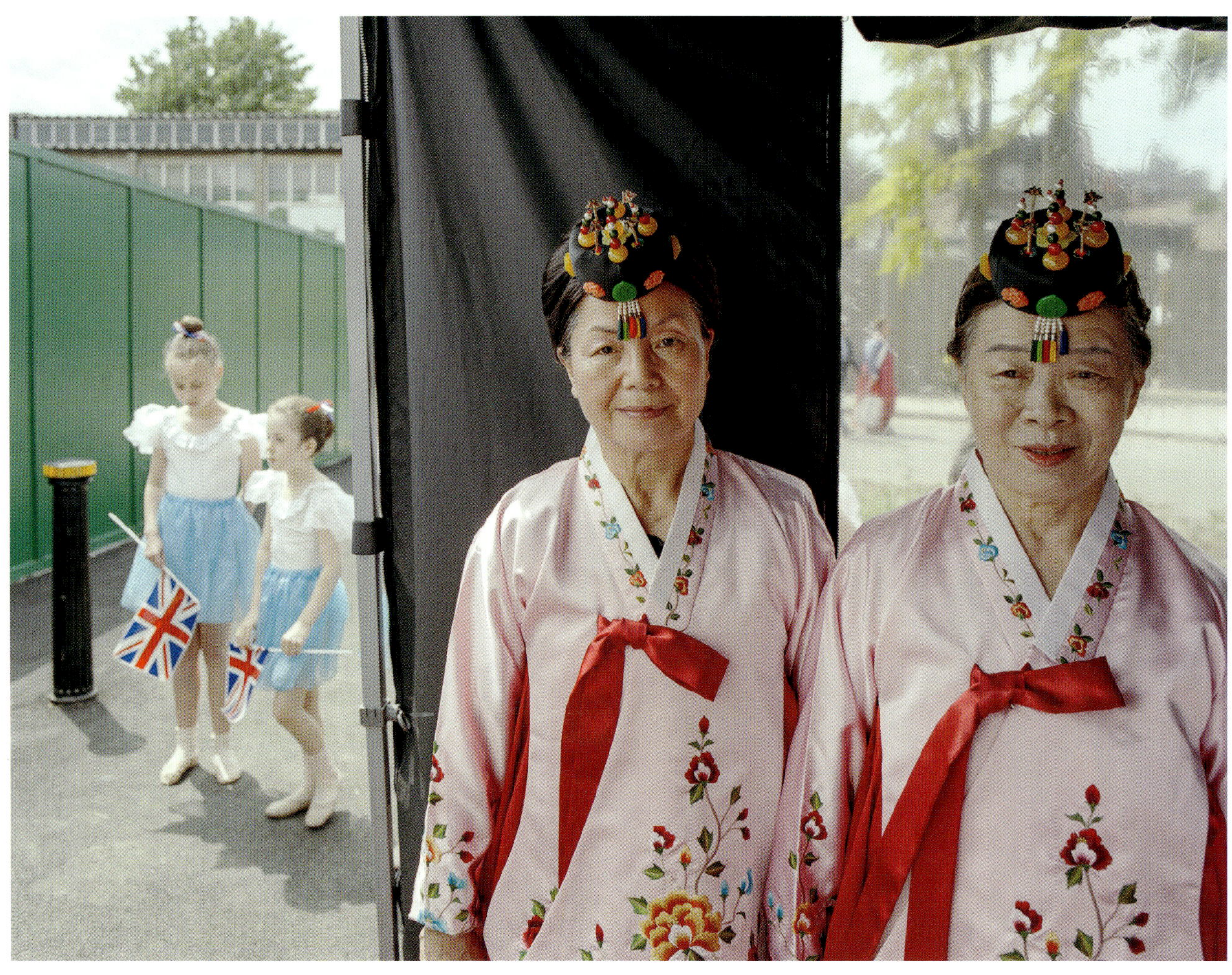

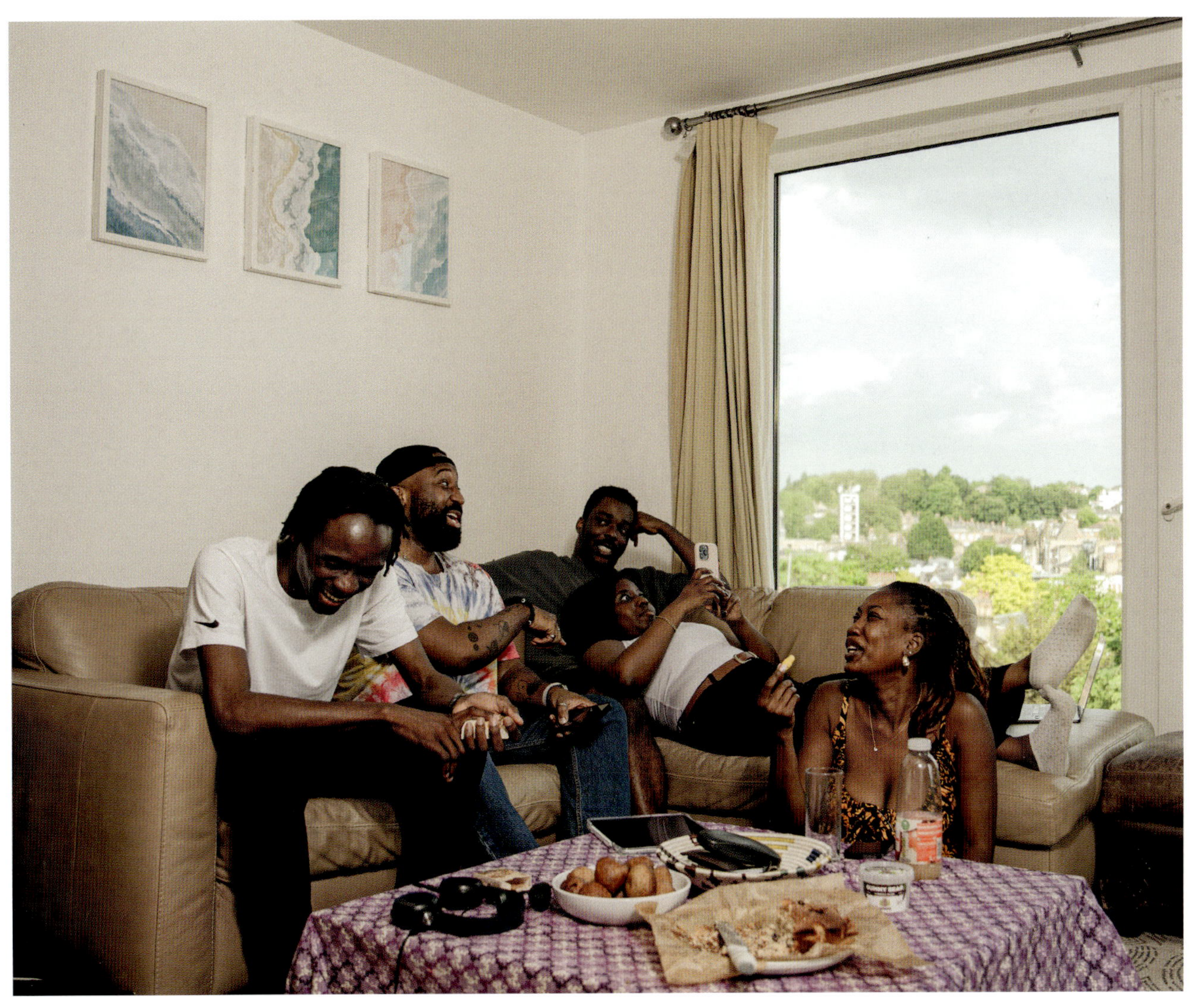

Iyesogie Ogieriakhi
Community, 2024
From the series *Welcome! You're Black*
Inkjet print

London-based photographer Iyesogie Ogieriakhi captures a fleeting moment of laughter amongst five Nigerians who relocated to the UK. A bowl of Nigerian puff puffs atop an Ankara printed tablecloth juxtaposes with the Deptford, London, skyline visible through the window. Ogieriakhi aims to bring focus to the complexities in navigating racial awareness and identity in a new environment, with this group portrait showing the universal need for community when far from home.

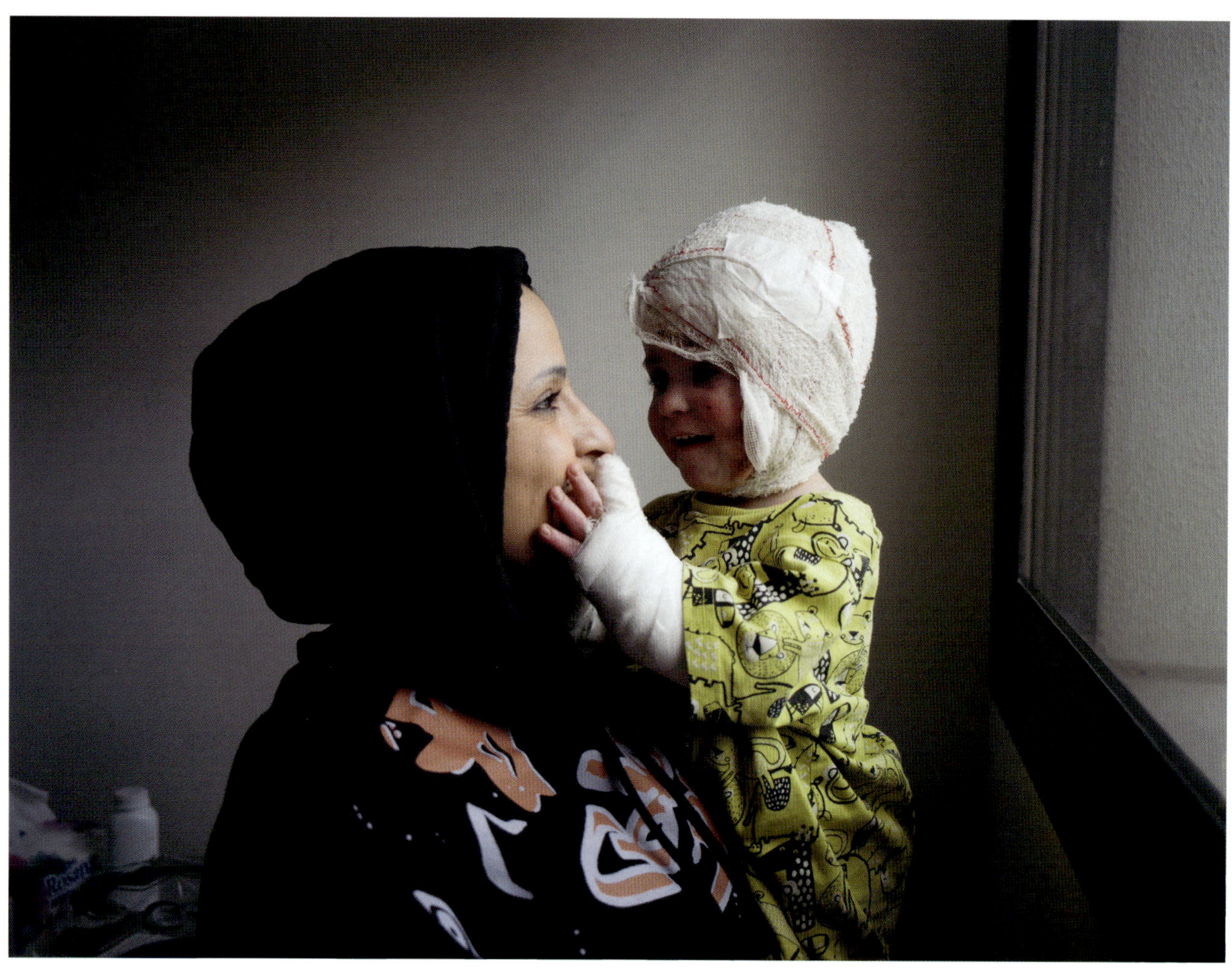

Giles Duley
Ivana and Fatima, 2024
Chromogenic print

This heartrending portrait of Ivana and her daughter Fatima was made two months after an Israeli-guided bomb hit the family's home in Lebanon. Ivana and her sister suffered severe burns and were left homeless; the family have since been supported by the No More War foundation, established by photographer Giles Duley in 2017. Himself a triple amputee following injuries sustained in Afghanistan, Duley's work documents the long-term impact of conflict on civilians. Despite incomprehensible suffering, a deep joy is visualised in the tender bond of mother and child.

William Sheepskin

The Farmhand's Son, 2024
From the series *On the Farm*
Inkjet print

Cape Town-based photographer William Sheepskin is drawn to the democratic nature of photography, particularly how small details can hold the attention of the viewer. The photographer encountered Vuyisanani wearing toy glasses while wandering along a farm road in the Eastern Cape of South Africa. Sheepskin felt moved by the boy's innocence and joy, qualities which allude to the intricacies of the lived experience in South Africa today. Sheepskin relocated to Tanzania and Mauritius during his childhood, and this migratory journey informs how he interprets the world around him.

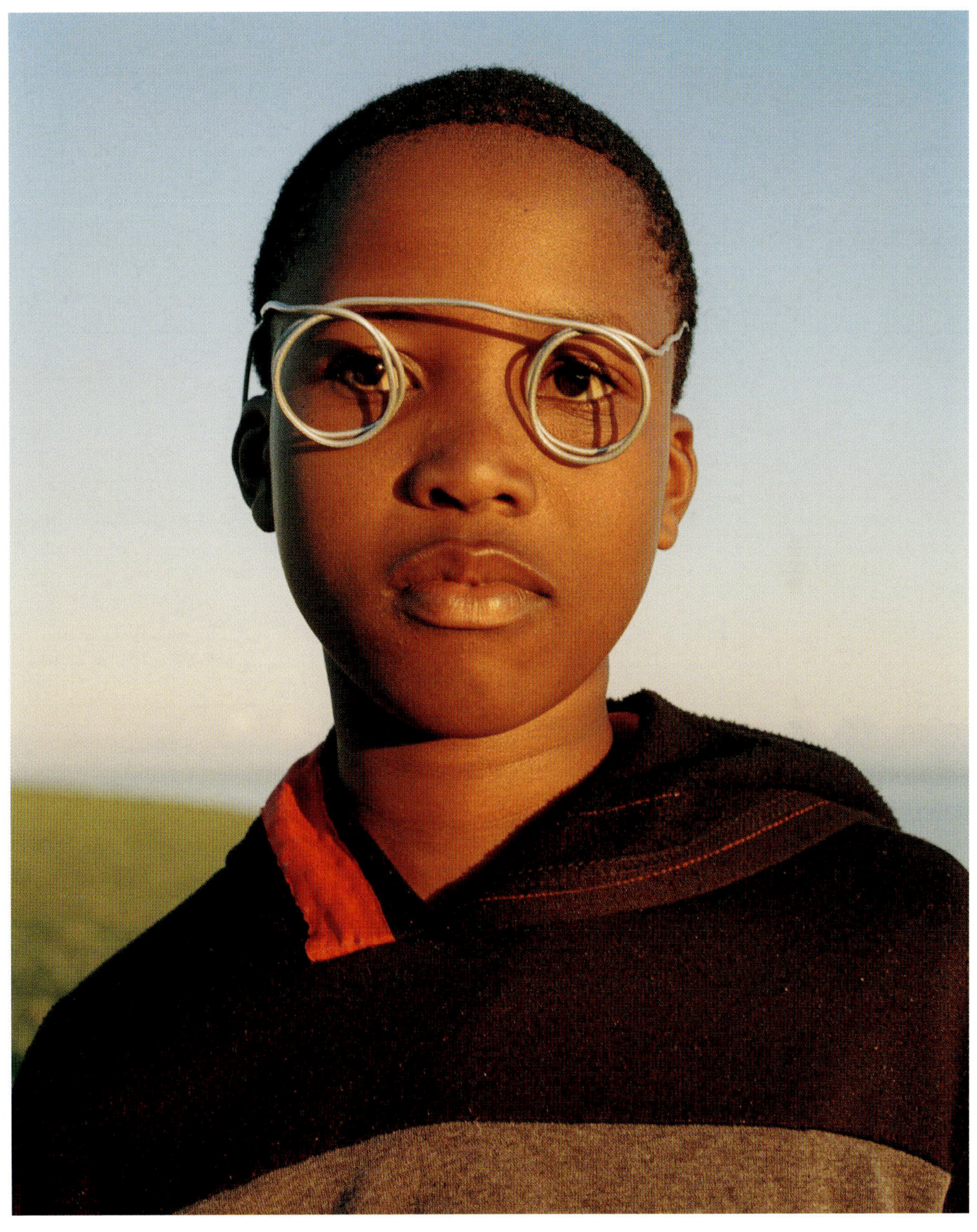

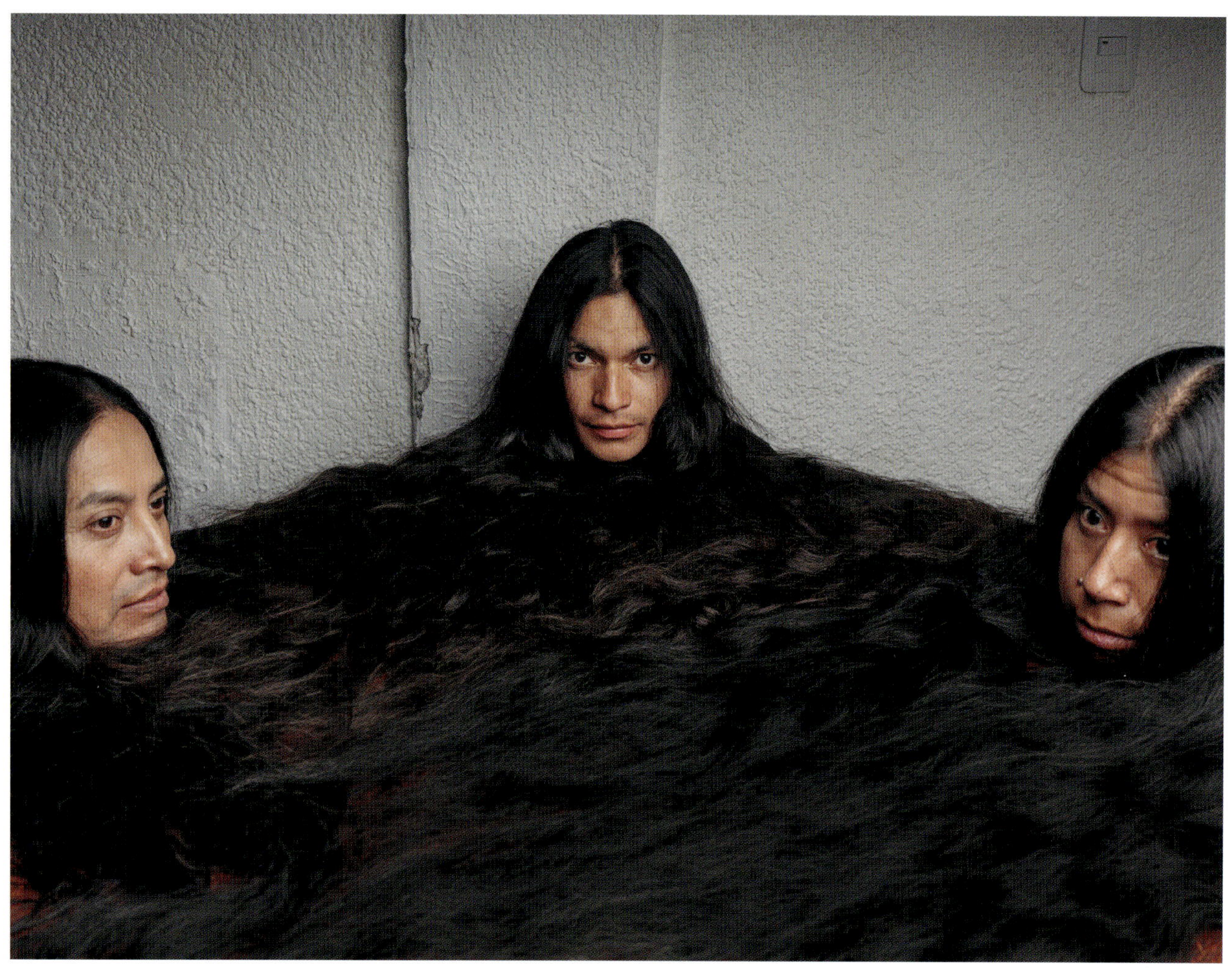

Irina Werning

Table of Hair, 2024
From the series *Las Pelilargas*
Chromogenic print

A sea of long hair dominates this triple portrait. Irina Werning arranges the sitters' hair across a table in Octavalo, Ecuador, where Kichwa men keep unshorn hair as a symbolic link to their ancestors and an extension of the self. The central figure looks out at the viewer, perhaps in resistance to the history of forced haircutting during the Spanish Inquisition. Inspired by Indigenous communities in her homeland, Argentinian photojournalist Werning has been photographing long hair since 2006.

David Vintiner

Alfie getting a haircut, 2024
From the series *Seven Minutes Minus*
Chromogenic print

British photographer David Vintier saw Alfie through the steamed-up windows of a barbershop and, drawn to the scene, immediately asked him and the owner if he could make this portrait. The normality and familiarity of this everyday scene of a young man having his hair cut is elevated; through the angled composition, positioning the viewer slightly above the sitter, and the stylistic austerity, with limited chromatic range, the portrait becomes subtle and suggestive.

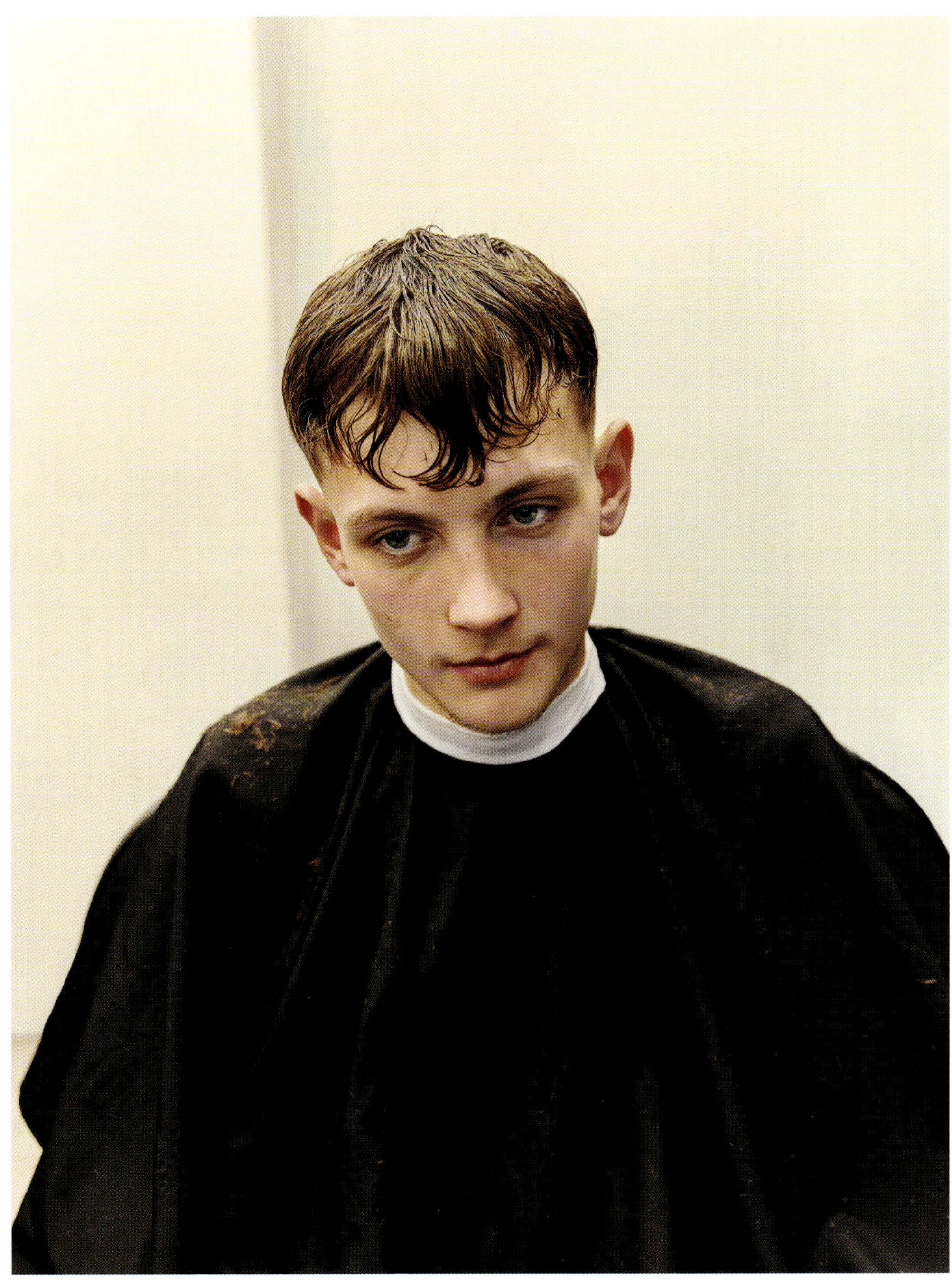

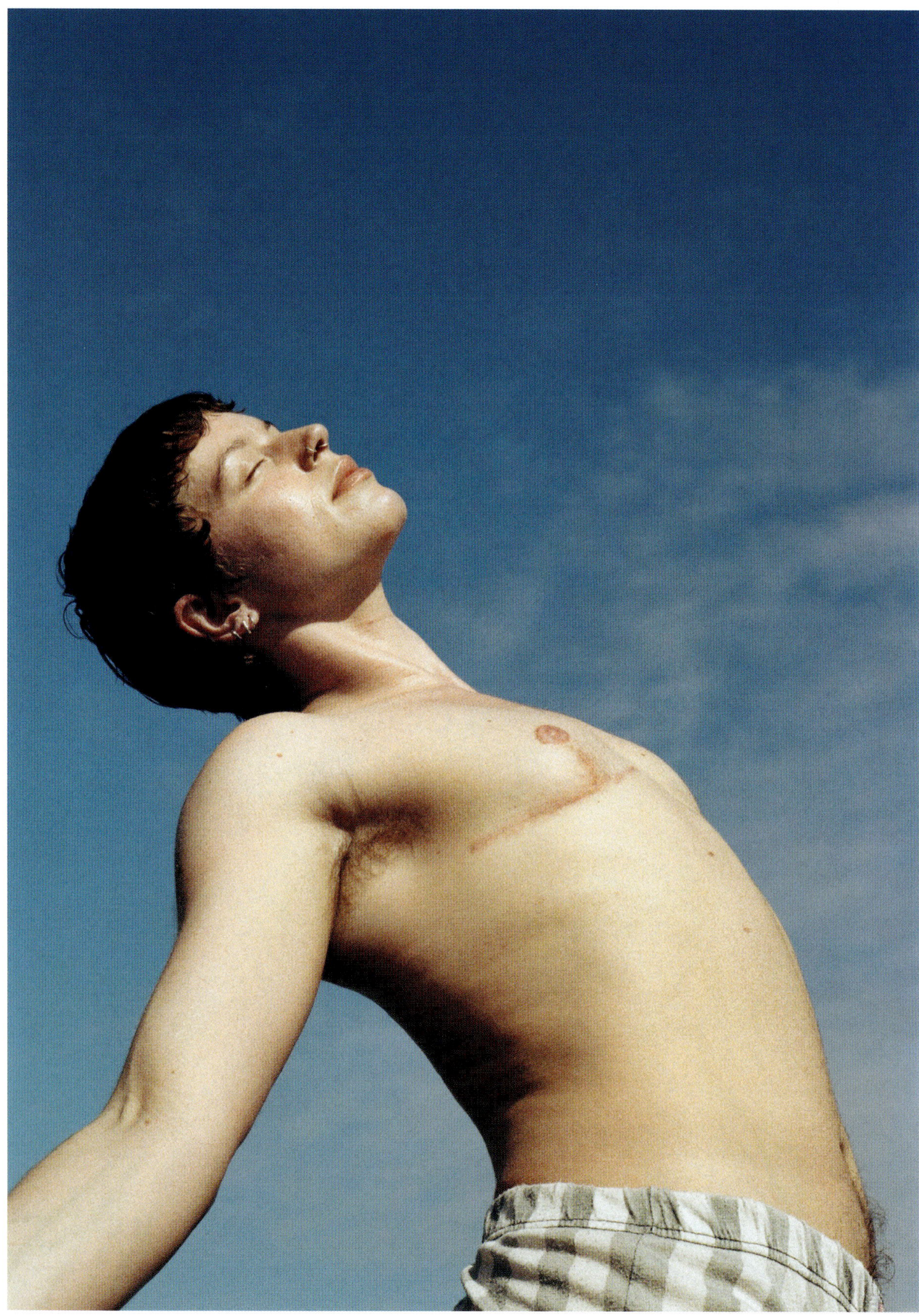

Pip Jay King

Freedom, 2025
From the series *At Home*
Inkjet print

Pip Jay King has been photographing Danni over the
last four years, following their personal journey as a
transgender and non-binary person. Danni's experience,
undergoing top surgery and masculinising hormone therapy,
is visualised in this moment of joy and serenity. Through
this documentation Danni is able to see themselves as King
does; 'at home in their body, radiating gender euphoria
on a spring day.' King's bodily details indicate a personal
passage which is captured in this image of liberation.

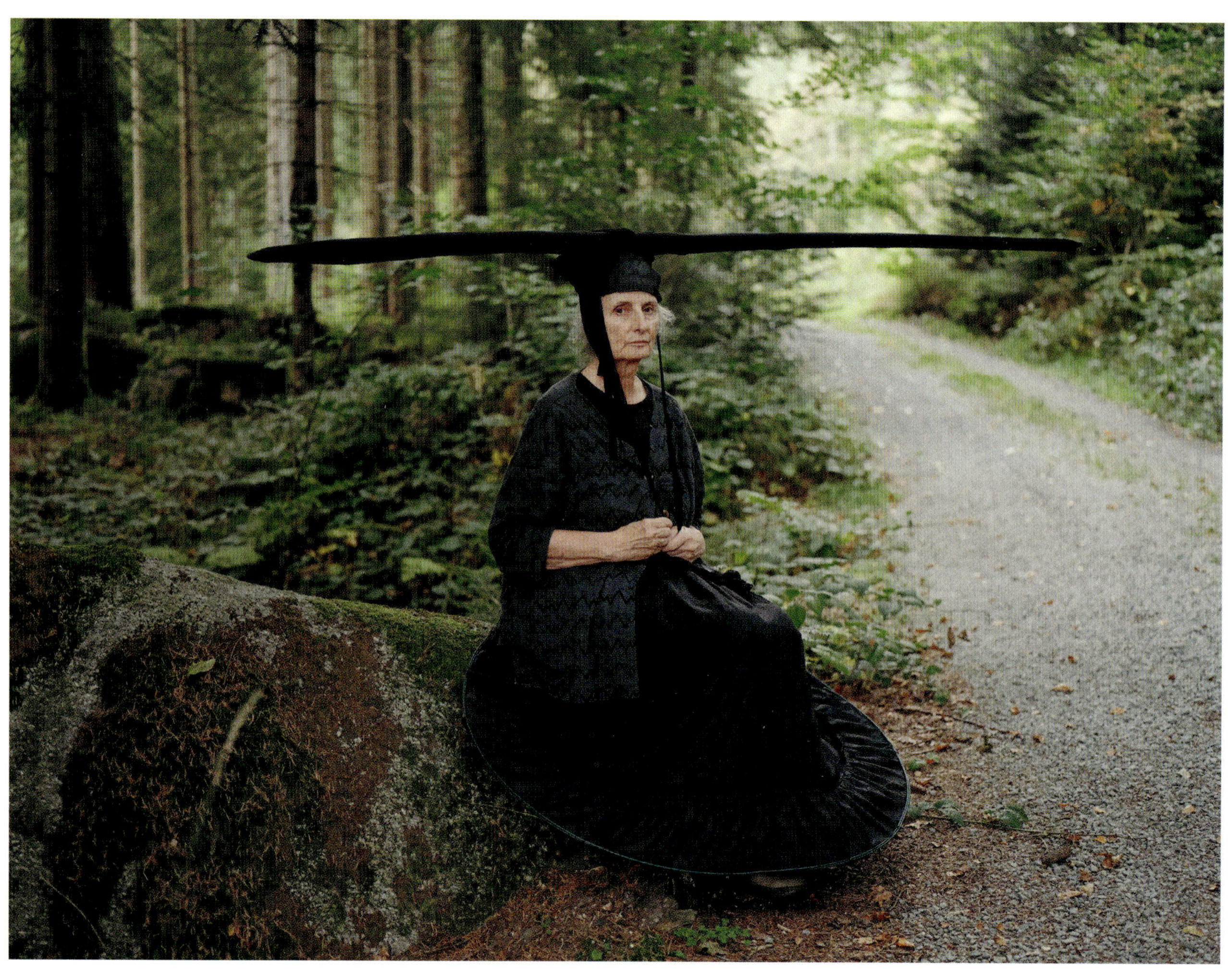

Camilla Greenwell
Gertraud Platschek, 2024
Chromogenic print

This portrait of artist Gertraud Platschek was taken in the forest near her home in Bavaria, Germany. Seated on a rock, Platschek is seen in one of her wearable works of sculpture, a hat made from a pole covered in black fabric. The horizontality of its form contrasts sharply with the natural environment, producing a 'glimmer' of the surreal which British photographer Camilla Greenwell often seeks out in her work. Greenwell's portrait, part documentation, part performance, was taken during a collaboration with Platschek.

Todd Antony

Buzkashi – Generations, 2025
From the series *Buzkashi*
Inkjet print

On a misty farm in the Sharistan District of Tajikistan, central Asia, Rusulov sits proudly on his horse. His piercing gaze holds attention amidst this richly detailed scene, while behind him a young Abdulqodir and his dog mimic the rider's pose. Forming part of a wider project on the centuries-old equestrian sport of Buzkashi, New Zealand-born photographer Todd Antony captures a moment of calm in the days leading up to a match involving over 300 riders.

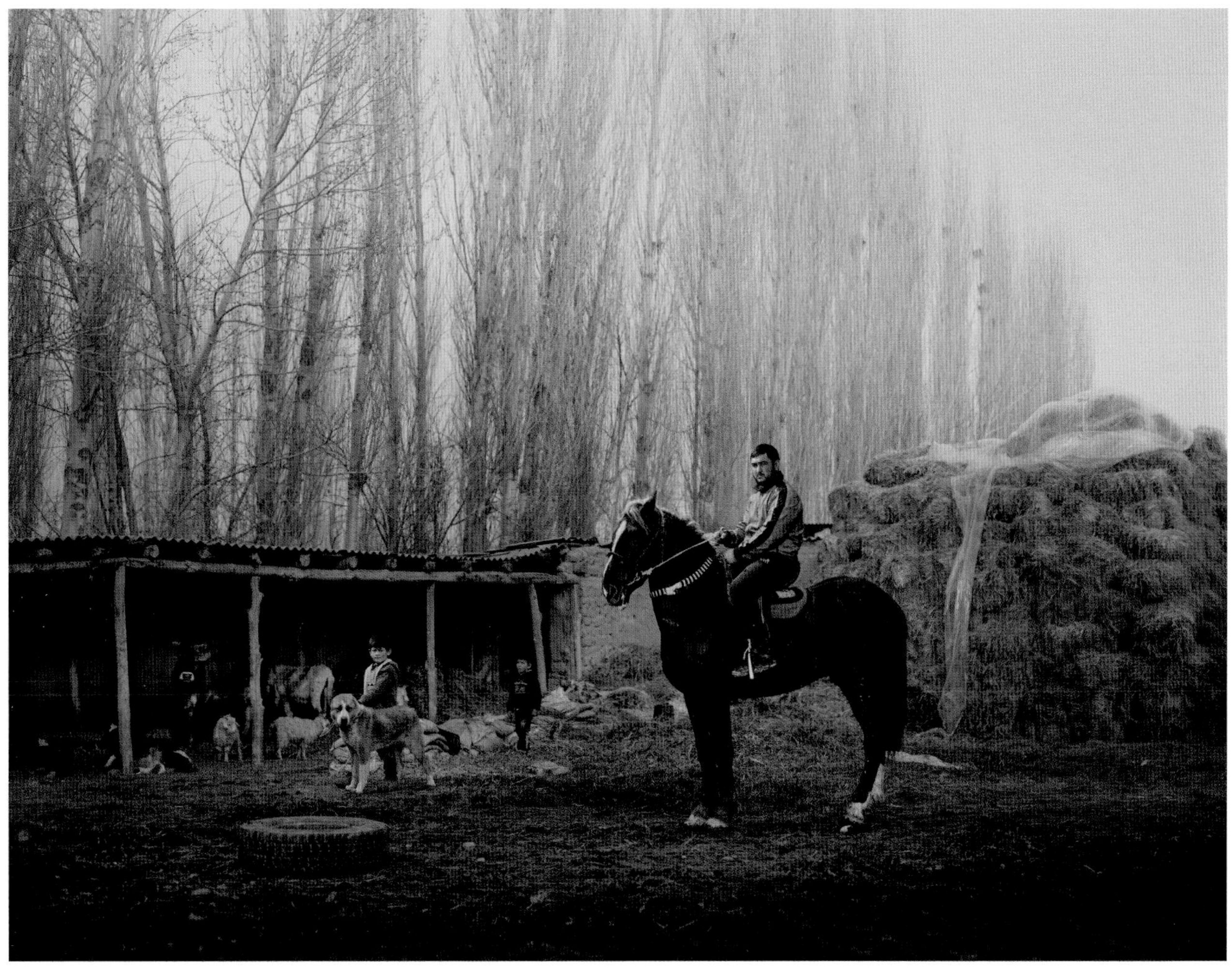

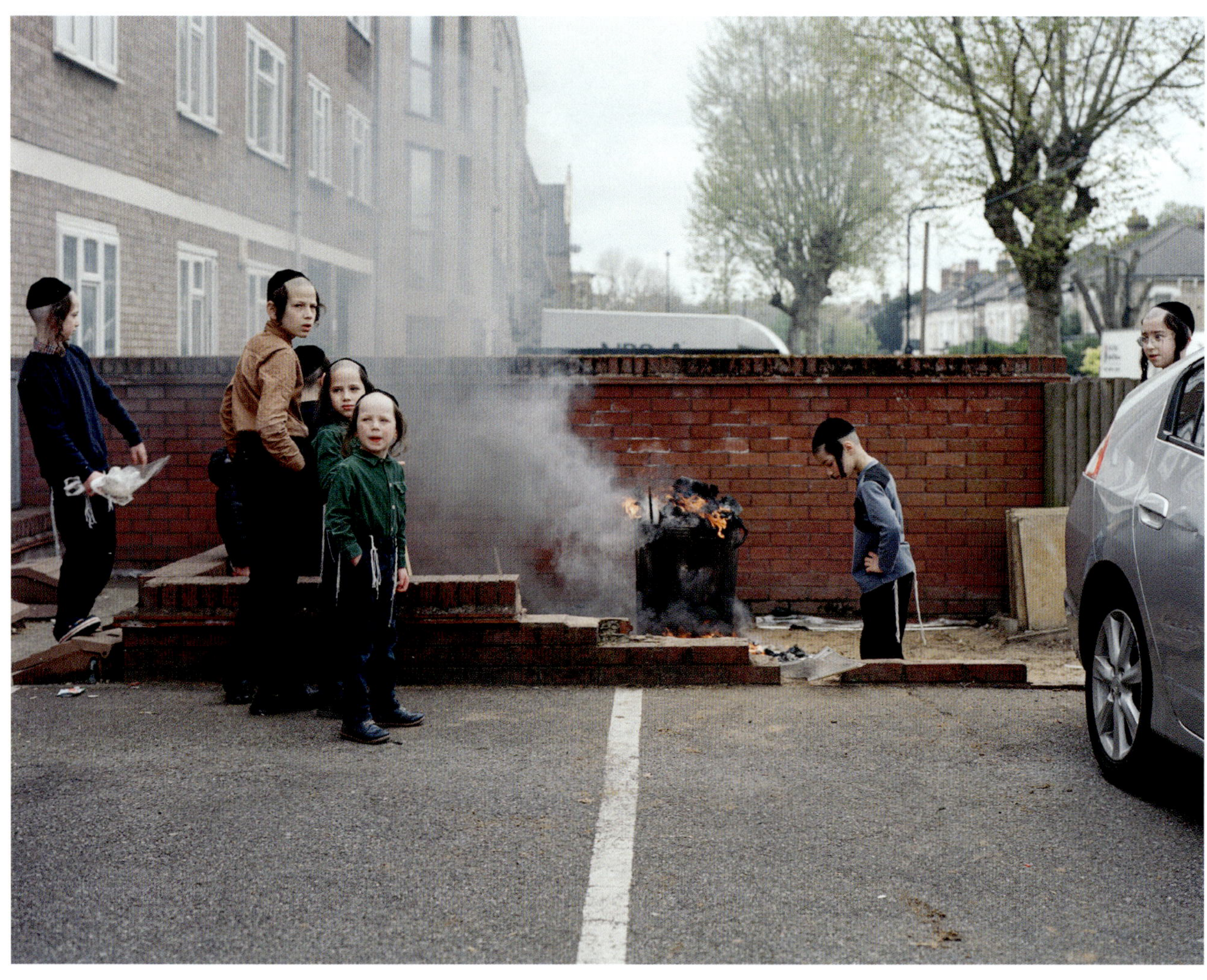

Francesco Fantini

Stamford Hill, 2024
From the series *London*
Inkjet print

In this dynamic street scene, Francesco Fantini depicts a group of Orthodox Jewish boys – his neighbours in Stamford Hill, North London – on the eve of the Passover holiday. They are burning *chametz*, leavened foods forbidden during Passover, as a symbolic and literal purging of leaven before the holiday begins. This image forms part of a wider body of work by the Italian, London-based photographer, documenting street life in the city.

JJ Keith

Zubeid, 2024
From the series *Open Britain: Portrait of a Diverse Nation*
Inkjet print

Zubeid stands amidst an all too familiar colour palette of white and seafoam green. He is wearing an NHS lanyard over a shalwar kameez (traditional Afghani dress), nearly indistinguishable from the hung lab coats occupying the background and foreground of the image. London-based photographer and filmmaker JJ Keith was inspired by the story of Zubeid's family – resettled refugees who fled the Afghan-Soviet War – to capture how essential migrants are to the NHS, as a vital part of the workforce. Zubeid's professional and personal identities blend seamlessly in this collaborative project with the NHS Imperial College Trust.

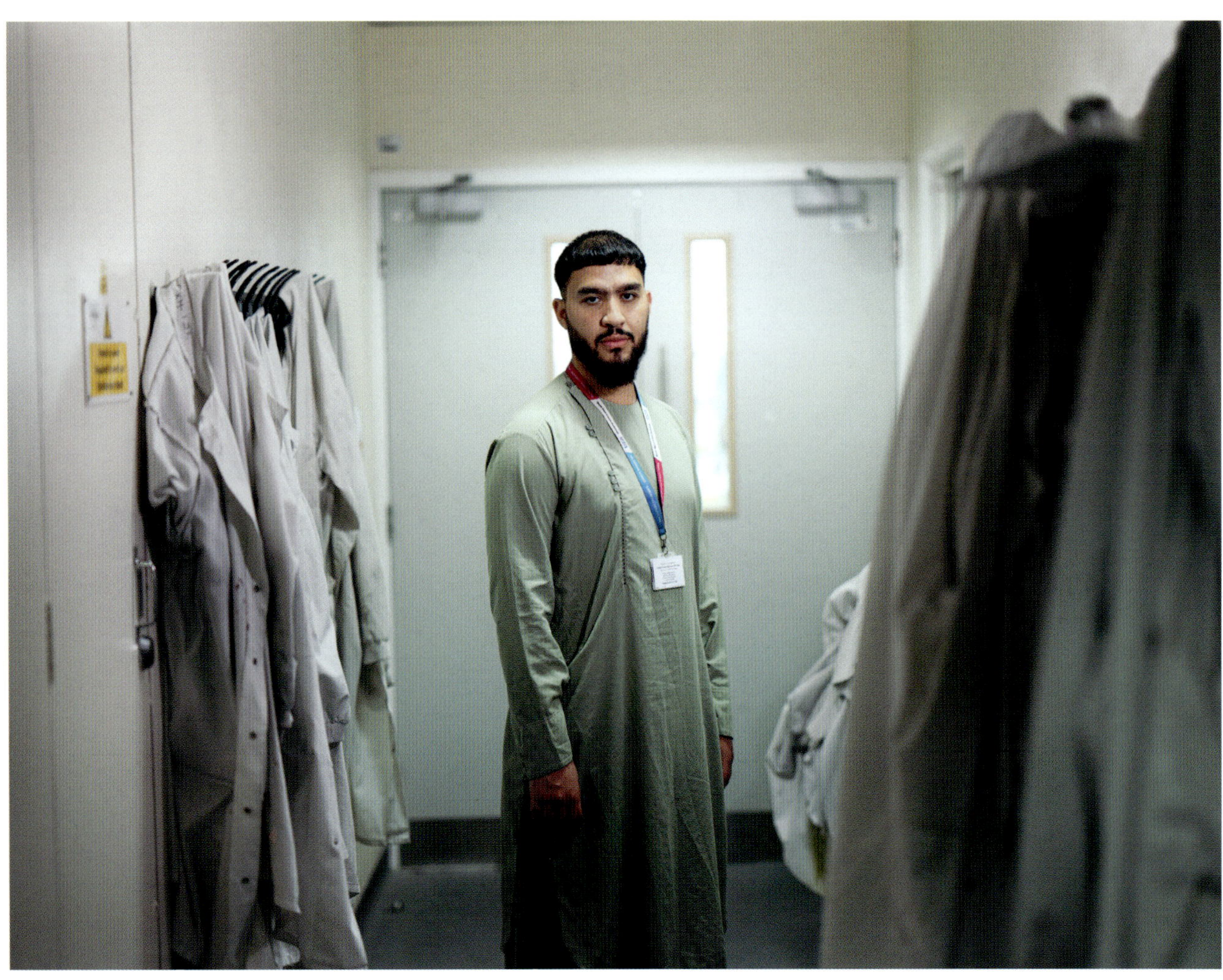

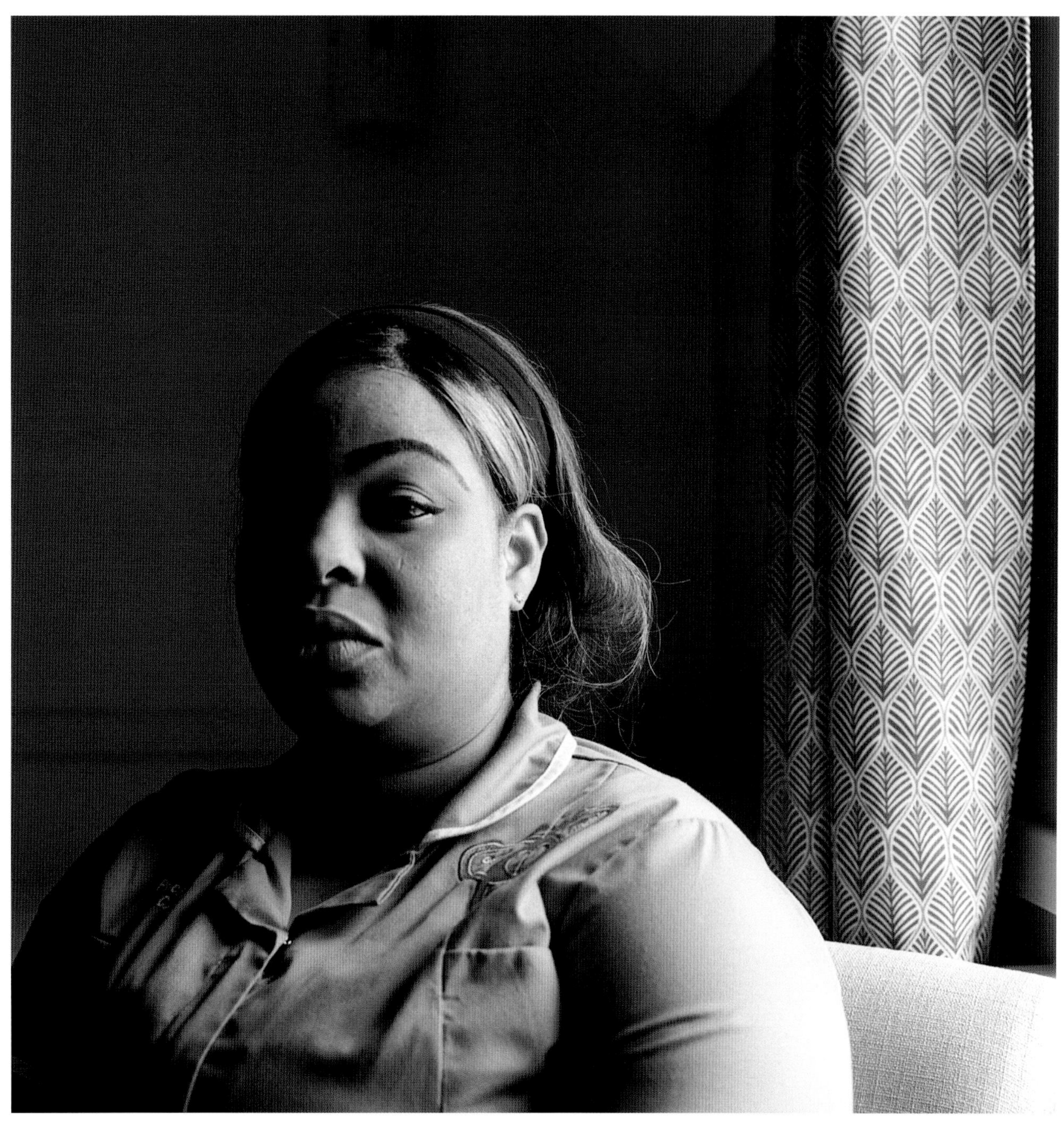

Daisy Moseley
Precious, 2024
From the series *Carers*
Gelatin silver print

This powerful portrait of Precious was taken in a care home in Yeovil, Somerset, and forms part of British photographer Daisy Moseley's series *Carers*. Begun in 2024, the project was inspired by the end of life care the photographer's mother provided for her grandmother. Moseley's series draws attention to the lack of support available 'to those caring for others on both a professional and personal level'; while highlighting the immense – and unseen – labour and value that they carry within society.

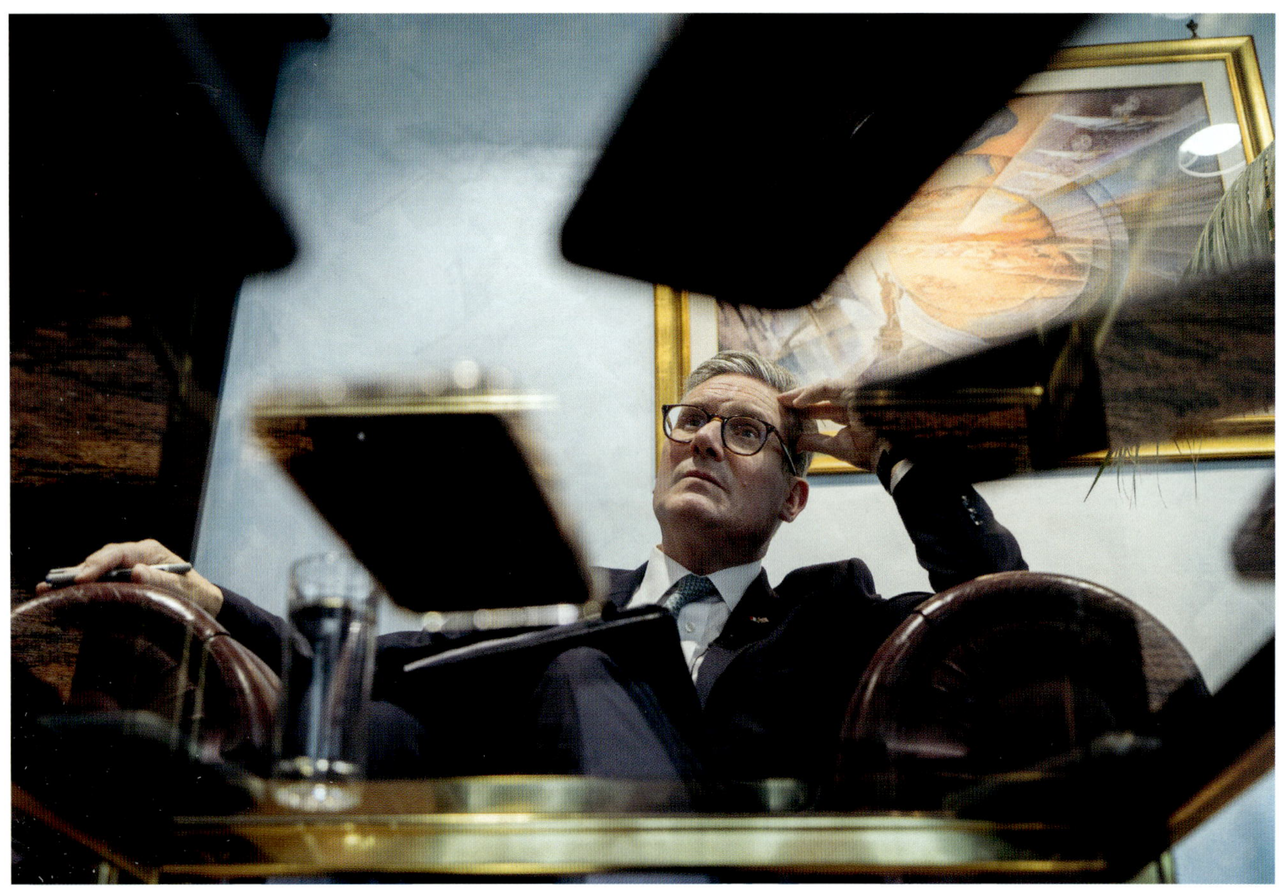

Harry Borden

Sir Keir Starmer, 2024
From the series *The First 100 Days of Labour*
Inkjet print

Portrait photographer Harry Borden provides an alternative vantage point from which to view the Prime Minister, so prominent in the public eye. Keir Starmer was fielding questions from journalists in 'the huddle'; their phones placed on the glass table to record answers. The shot was taken just before Starmer boarded a plane from Rome where he committed to cross-border collaboration to reduce illegal migration. Borden captured an intimate account of the first 100 days of the Labour administration for the *Guardian* newspaper.

Dominic Whisson

Owen Cooper, 2025
From the series *The Threshold*
Chromogenic print

Star of Netflix series *Adolescence* (2025), 15-year-old
Owen Cooper is captured at the breakthrough of his
career and in the midst of his own adolescence. British
photographer Dominic Whisson chooses a traditional,
studio setting for this portrait replete with a blue backdrop
and chair for the sitting. Yet, Cooper gazes absently into
the distance as if unaware of the camera. Whisson's portrait
interrogates the space between subject and symbol,
representation and reality; Cooper's existence in the
image references both the weight of the fictional show
he was a part of and the pressing reality of its narrative.

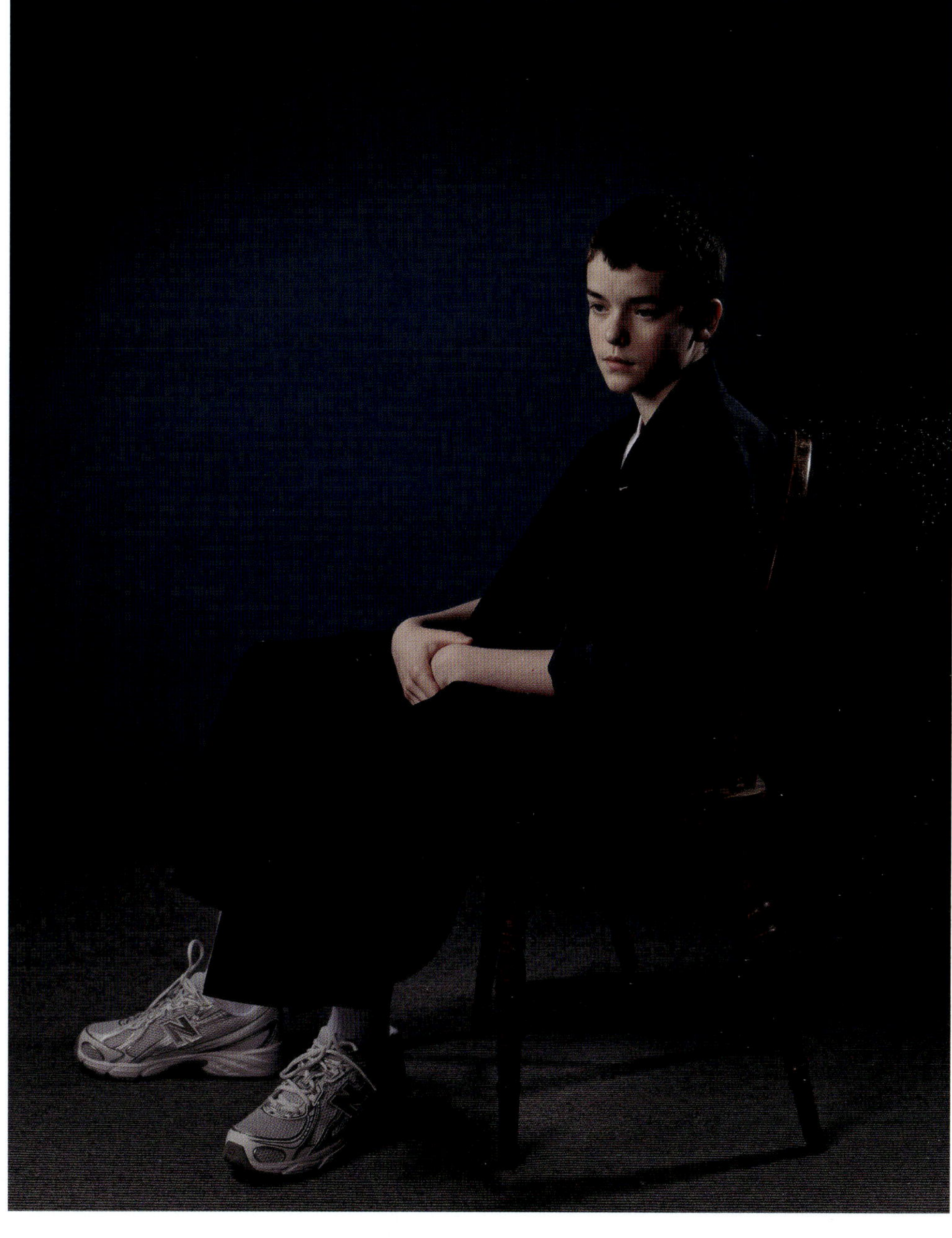

Chris O'Donovan

Sarah and Rachel, 2025
Inkjet print

Pictured here in Pentecostal dress after a Sunday service,
Sarah (left) and her cousin Rachel share a warm embrace,
illuminated by the golden light streaming in through the
church window. Rachel's smart watch adds a touch of
modernity to this otherwise timeless image. Rachel invited
British photographer Christopher O'Donovan to visit her
church in their local area of Elephant and Castle. The
portrait forms part of O'Donovan's ongoing exploration of
south London communities and the spaces they gather in.

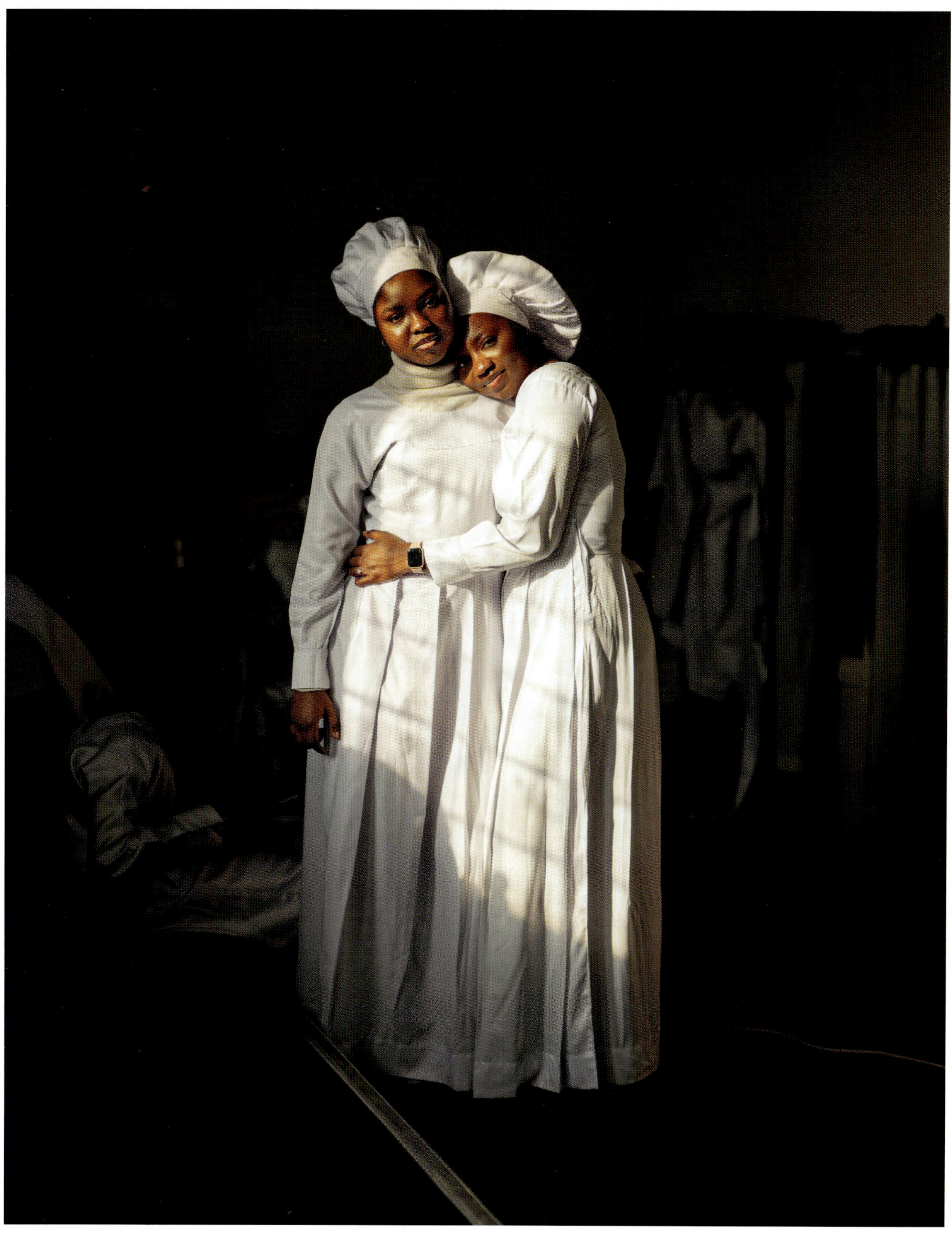

Anastasia Taylor-Lind

Tymofii, 2024
From the series *5k from the Frontline*
Inkjet print

British-Swedish photojournalist Anastasia Taylor-Lind has documented the life of Tymofii and his family since 2018, when they lived in Avdiivka, Ukraine. With Russia's invasion in February 2022, and the occupation of Avdiivka by Russian forces, the family have been displaced. The portrait is part of a project about everyday life in the region of Donbas during the conflict, produced in collaboration with anthropologist and journalist Alisa Sopova. Exemplified in this powerful portrait, *5k from the Frontline* focuses on the realities of living through military violence.

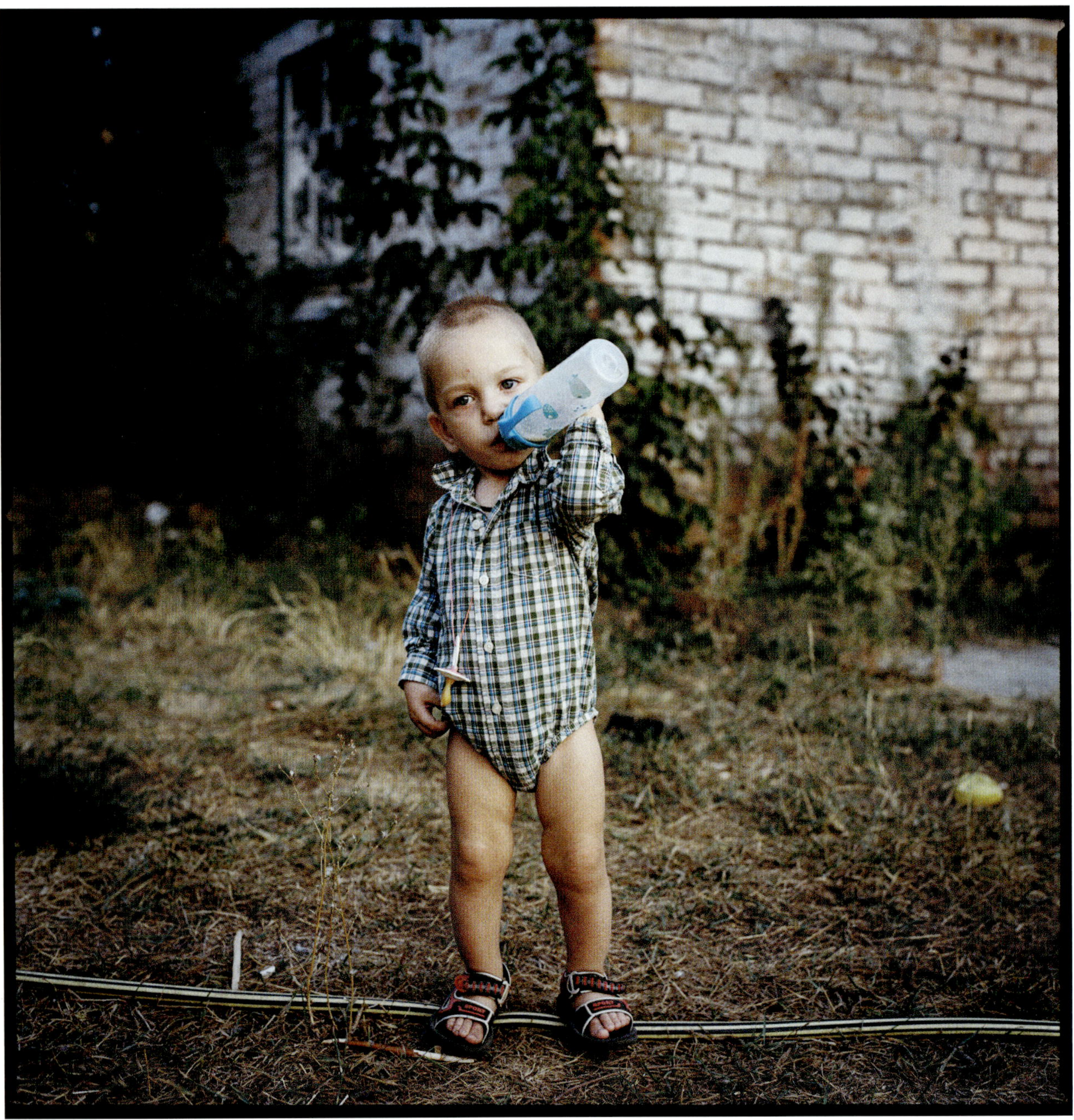

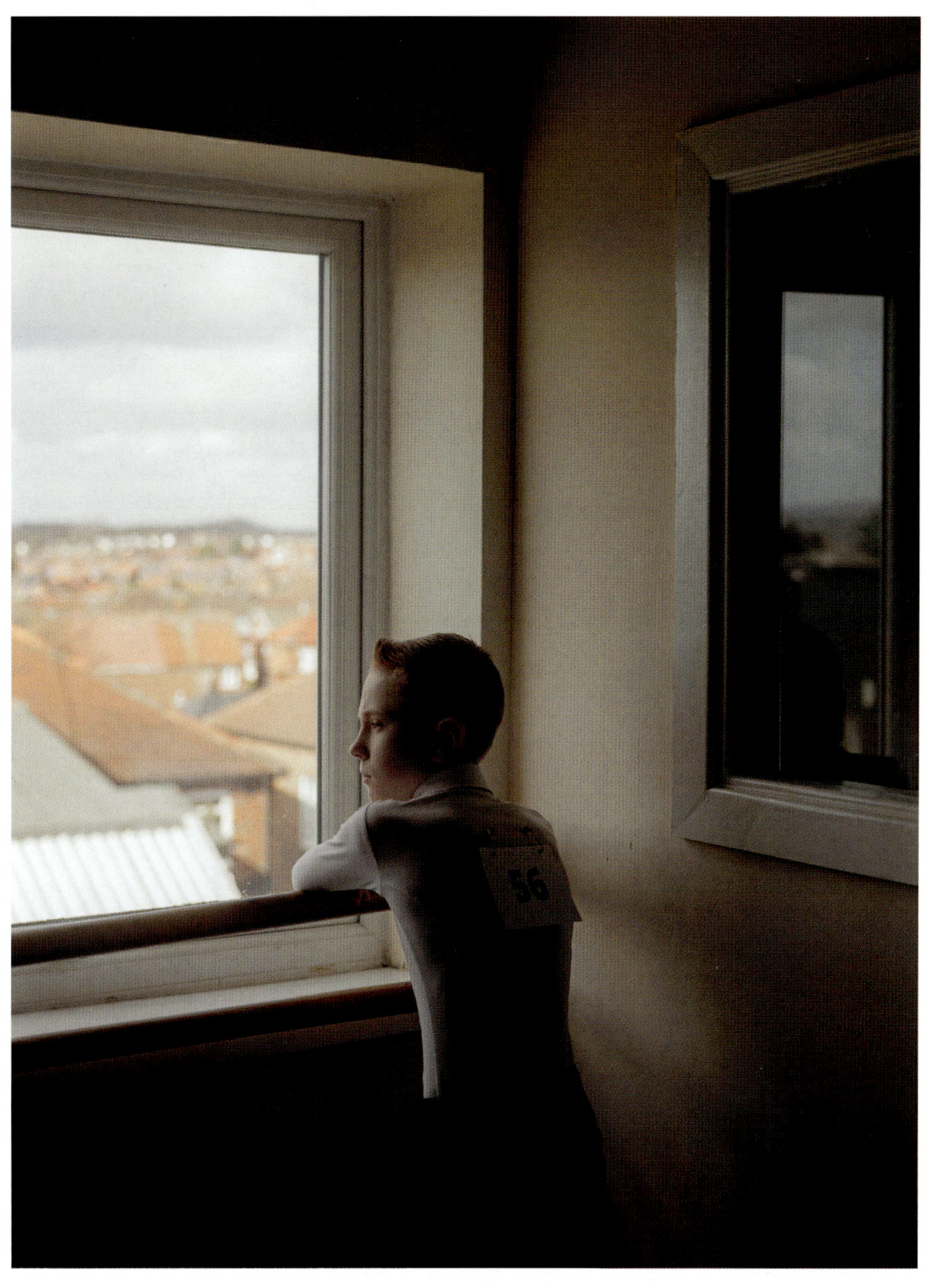

Christopher Owens
Abe, 2024
Inkjet print

This portrait, by British photographer Christopher Owens, captures a moment of stillness in a dance studio, as the sitter looks out of the window over the red rooftops of Newcastle's west end. The sitter, Abe, has had a passion for ballroom dancing from a young age, but frequently contends with hurtful stereotypes. Challenging outdated notions of masculinity, Owens's portrait conveys the quiet determination which can be seen in the sitter's face.

Steve Reeves

Allana, 2025
From the series *Before We Were Proud*
Inkjet print

Allana appears strong but reflective, standing in an
ordinary suburban street. Her portrait forms part of Steve
Reeve's moving tribute to older members of the LGBTQ+
community, who were living before the decriminalisation
of homosexuality in the UK in 1967. Allana transitioned ten
years ago, after living much of her adult life suffering from
depression from gender dysphoria and only finding inner
peace when underwater as a Navy diver. 'Becoming who
I truly am has been, in short, nothing but hard, hard work',
she says.

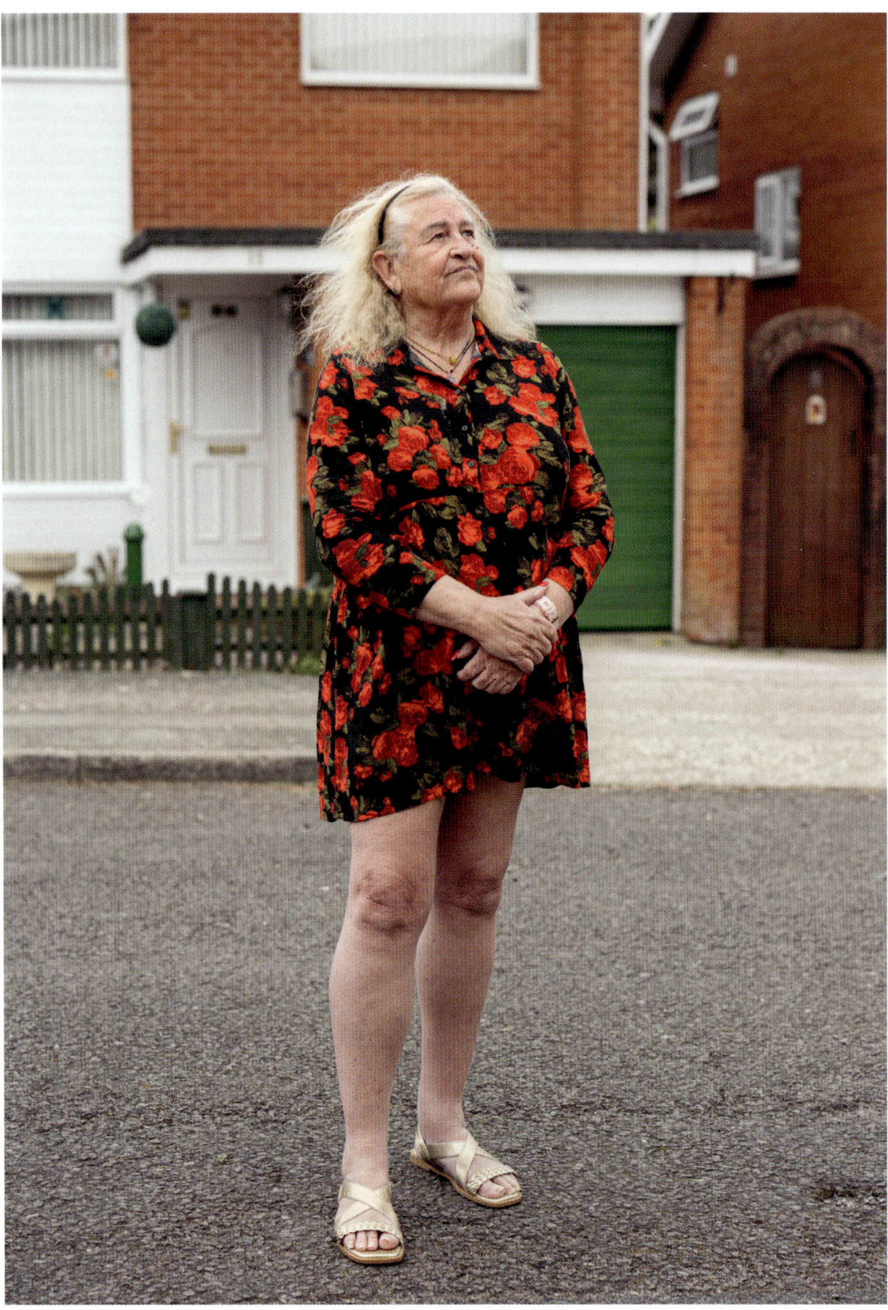

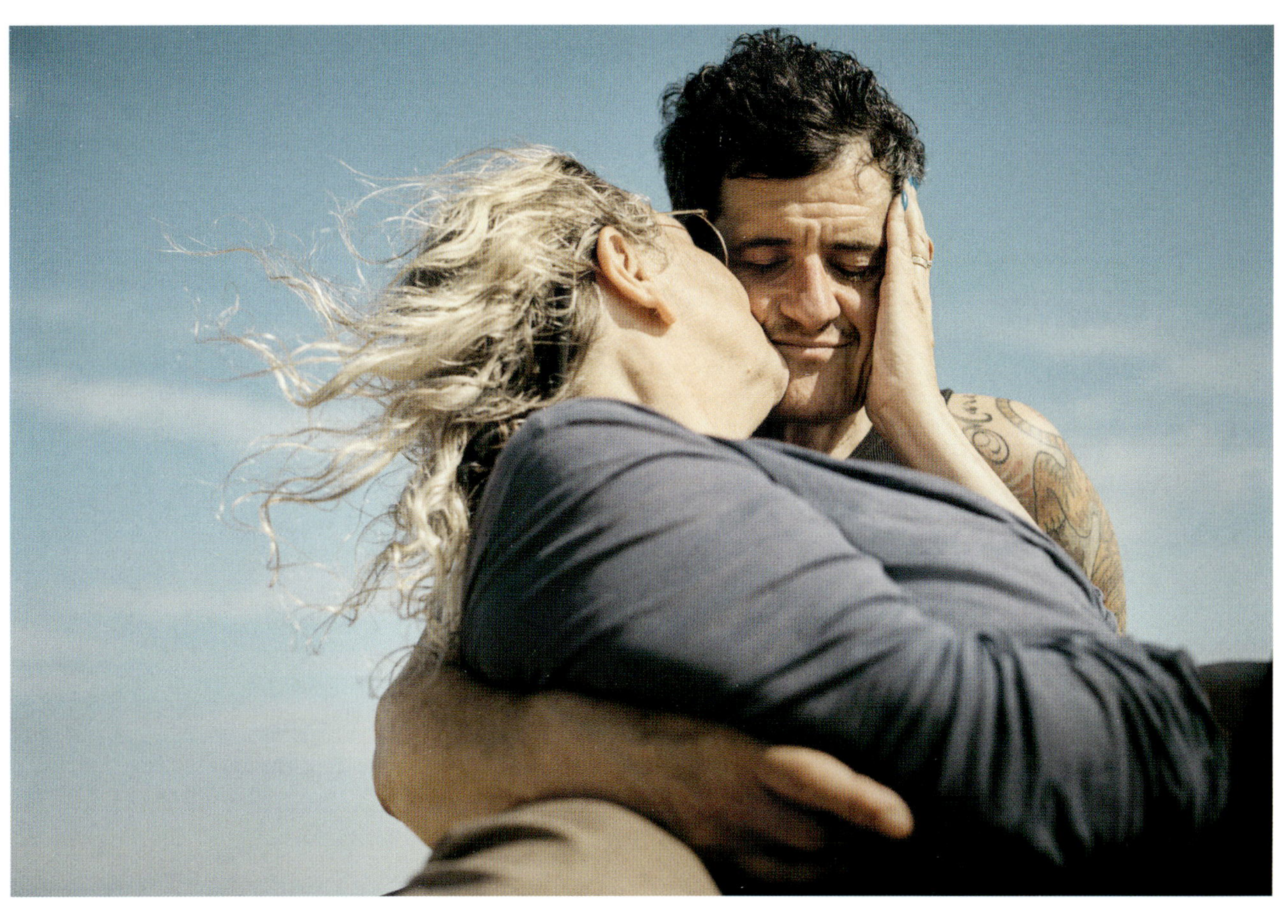

Olly Burn
Jules and Marie, 2024
Chromogenic print

A tender moment is captured as if neither subject is aware of the camera. Jules and Marie are friends of photographer Olly Burn, who captures this warm, candid scene on the beach in Hove, east Sussex. It celebrates the diversity within straight passing queer couples.
As viewers, we become party to this intimate celebration of their freedom to embrace in the open and to challenge stereotypical gender roles.

Roman Manfredi
Elizabeth, 2024
From the series *Fair Play*
Gelatin silver print

Elizabeth is pictured as part of Roman Manfredi's environmental portrait project *Fair Play*; it focuses on Clapton Community Football Club's women and non-binary development and reserves teams. Shot on medium format, this dignified portrait explores themes of equity and solidarity through the power of grassroots community engagement. Harmoniously composed at the member-owned grounds in east London, Manfredi captures the banners hung on the modest stands that attest to the club's principles of inclusivity and activism.

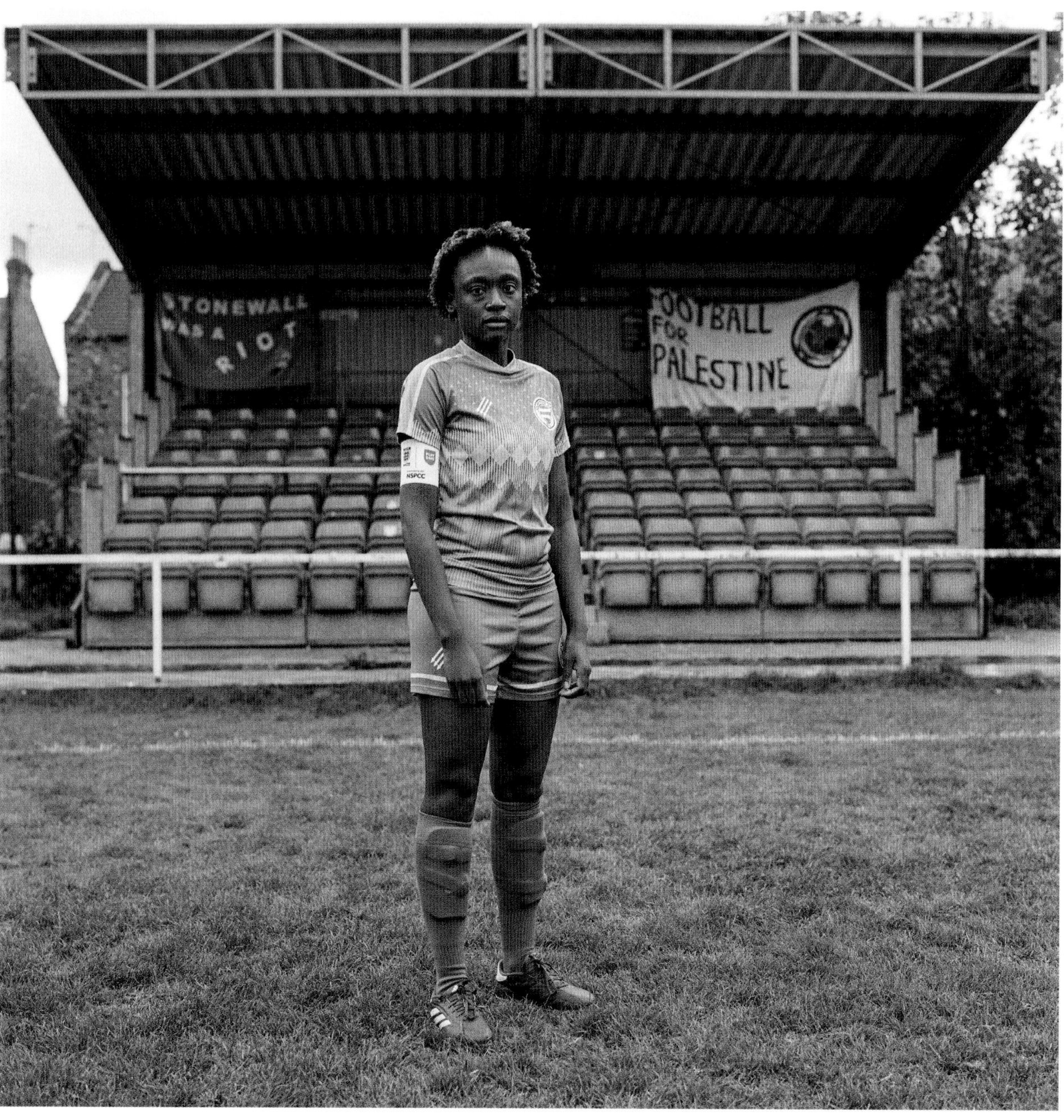

Roman Manfredi
Elizabeth, 2024
From the series *Fair Play*
Gelatin silver print

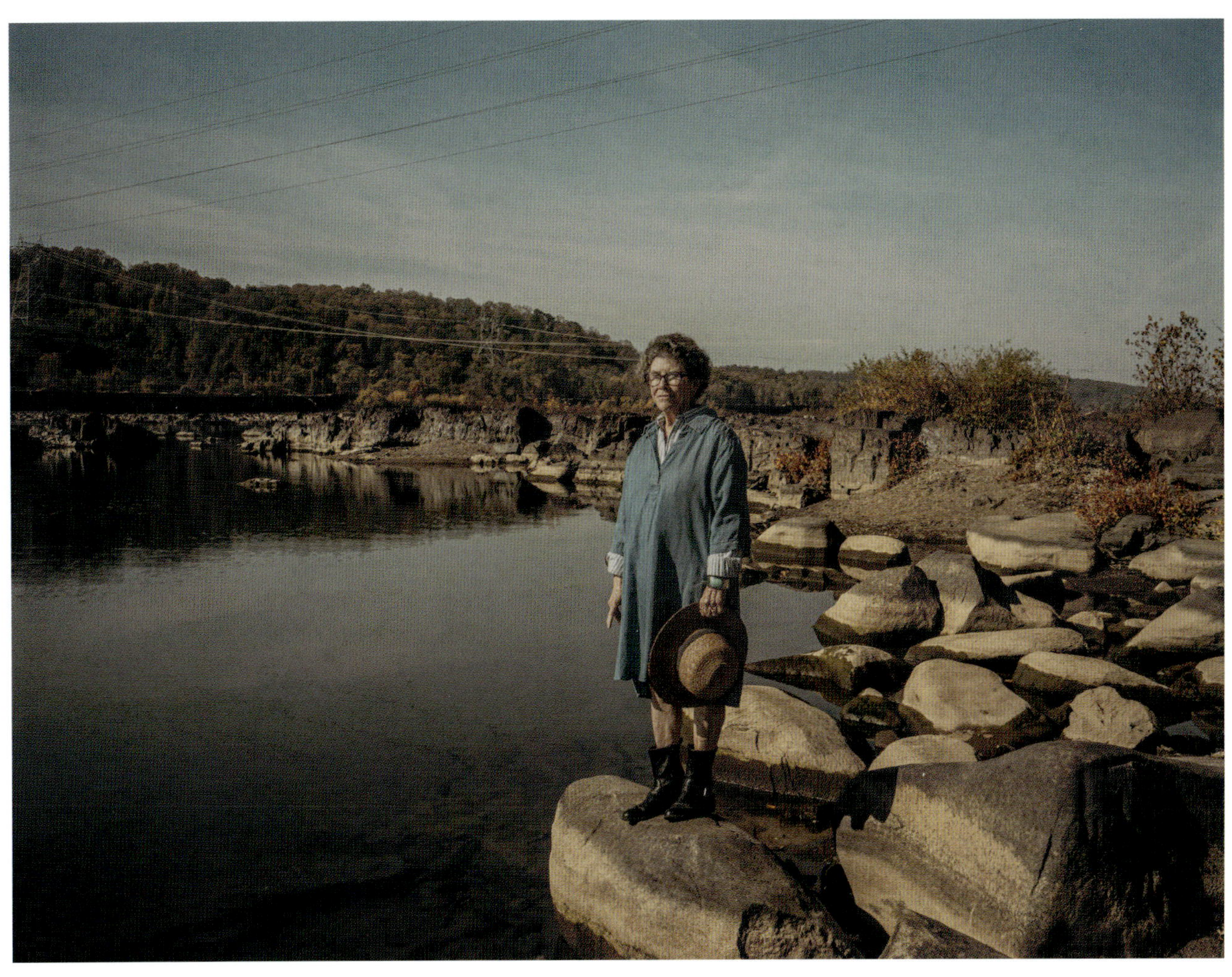

Greg Kahn
Three Mile Island, 2024
Chromogenic print

Wearing a loose denim dress and straw hat in hand, Patricia Longenecker stands confidently in a rocky landscape near a river. She was a farmer living three miles away from the 1979 Three Mile Island accident in Pennsylvania – the worst accident in USA commercial nuclear power plant history. Forced to evacuate with her family, Longenecker now feels 'betrayed' by plans to reopen the site. American photographer Greg Khan explored this complex subject for the *Financial Times*.

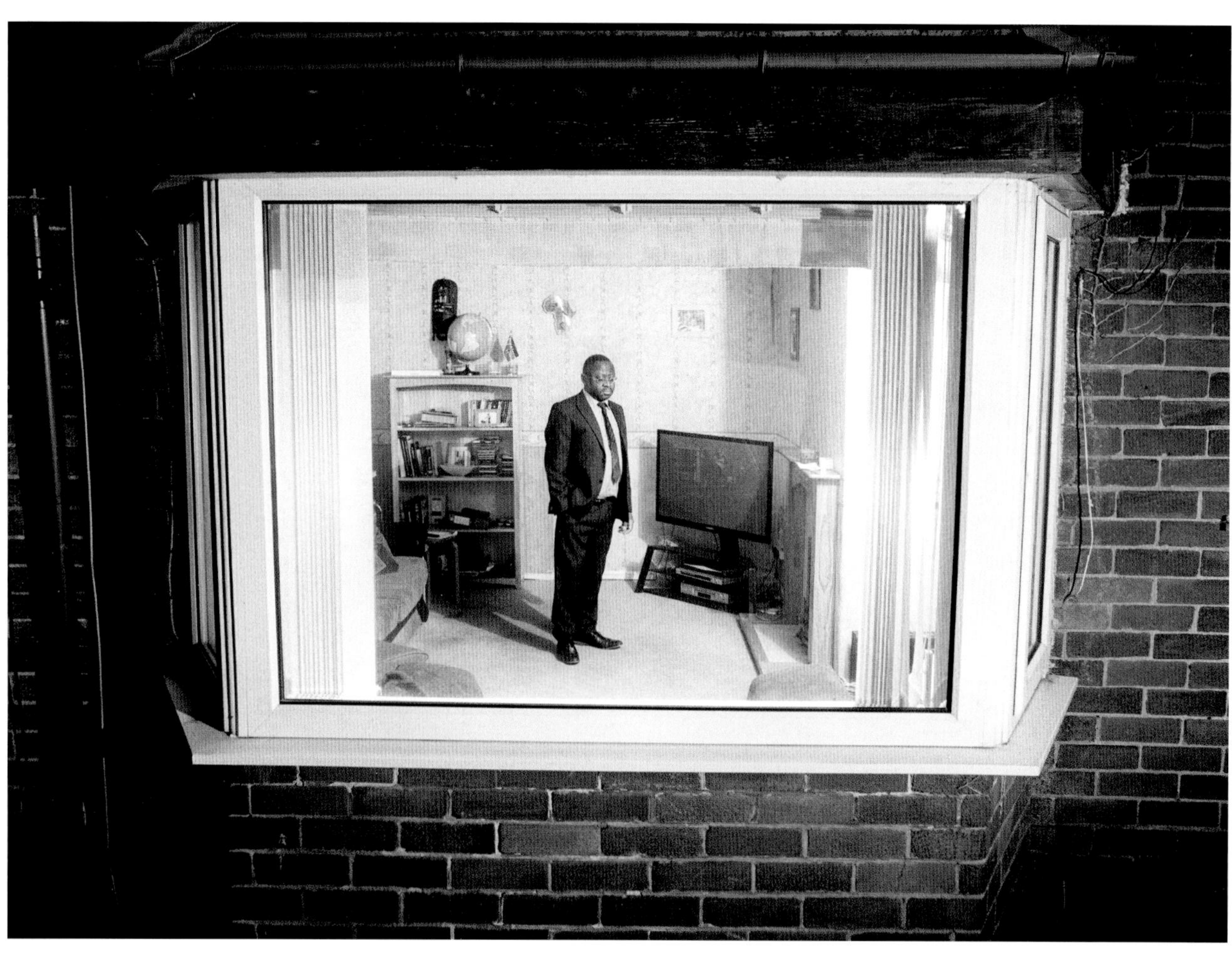

Timon Benson

About to Leave, 2024
From the series *Father*
Inkjet print

About to Leave is part of a project documenting the relationship between the photographer, Manchester-born Timon Benson, and his father, John. Pictured standing in his living room, John is twice framed: first by the window, second by the lens. The work is a reflection on their family's migration to the UK and John's decision to return to Kenya after 34 years. On arrival he had worn his own father's suit, here he wears his tie. Benson's portrait presents a powerful image of time, memory and family.

Agata Szymanowicz
Blended Identity, 2025
Chromogenic print

Gathered in the front garden of their parents-in-laws' house in London, Polish-born family photographer Agata Szymanowicz turns the camera towards her own family. She pictures herself to the far left wearing a Poland football scarf, next to her Glaswegian husband sporting a Celtic F.C. shirt and kilt. Szymanowicz's brother-in-law's family are to the right, anchored by the first-generation Bangladeshi grandparents at the centre. This untraditional family portrait, featuring a mix of ethnicities, personal styles and children from previous relationships, reflects the diversity of families in Britain today composed of blended identities from the individual to the collective.

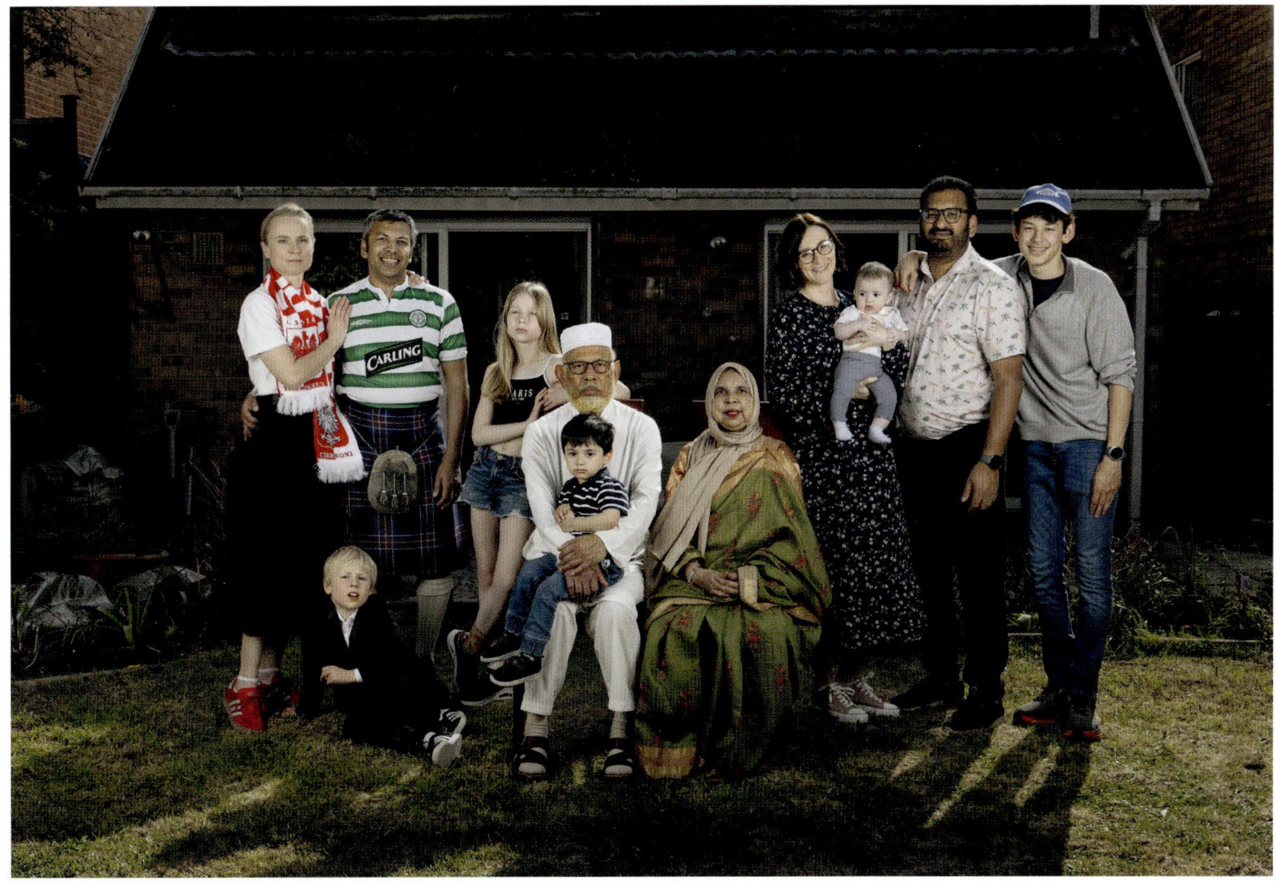

Juliet Klottrup
Molly and Amber, 2024
From the series *Skate Like a Lass*
Chromogenic print

Taken from the series *Skate Like a Lass*, a project that documents inclusive grassroots skateboarding communities in the north of England, this portrait shows 9-year-olds Molly and Amber at a Girls' Skate Night. British visual artist Juliet Klottrup collaborates with skaters to create 'a co-authored archive addressing the gaps in representation, participation, and historical documentation within skateboarding'. Klottrup's portraits present these skate parks as spaces of belonging, self-expression and connection.

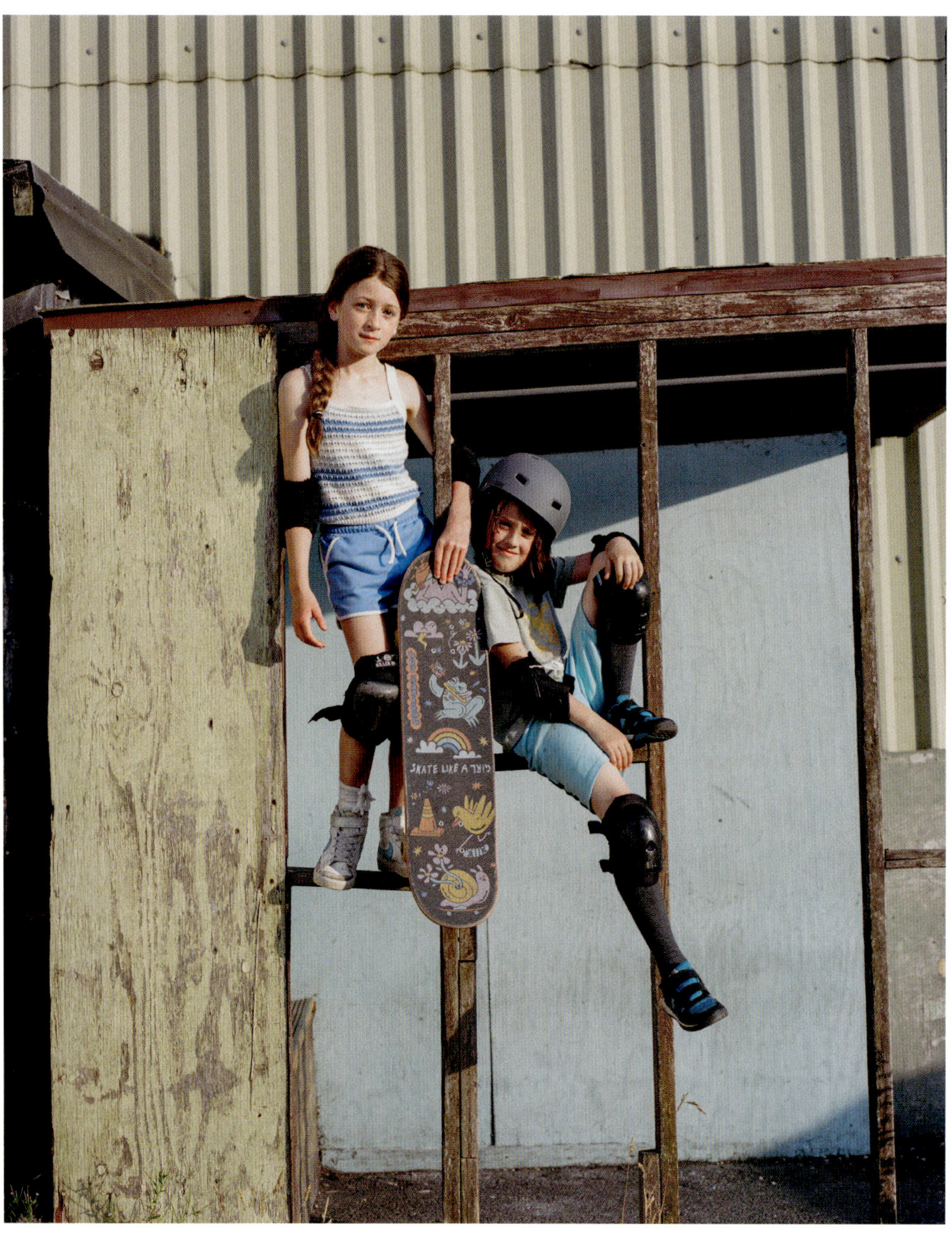

Juliet Klottrup
Molly and Amber, 2024
From the series *Skate Like a Lass*
Chromogenic print

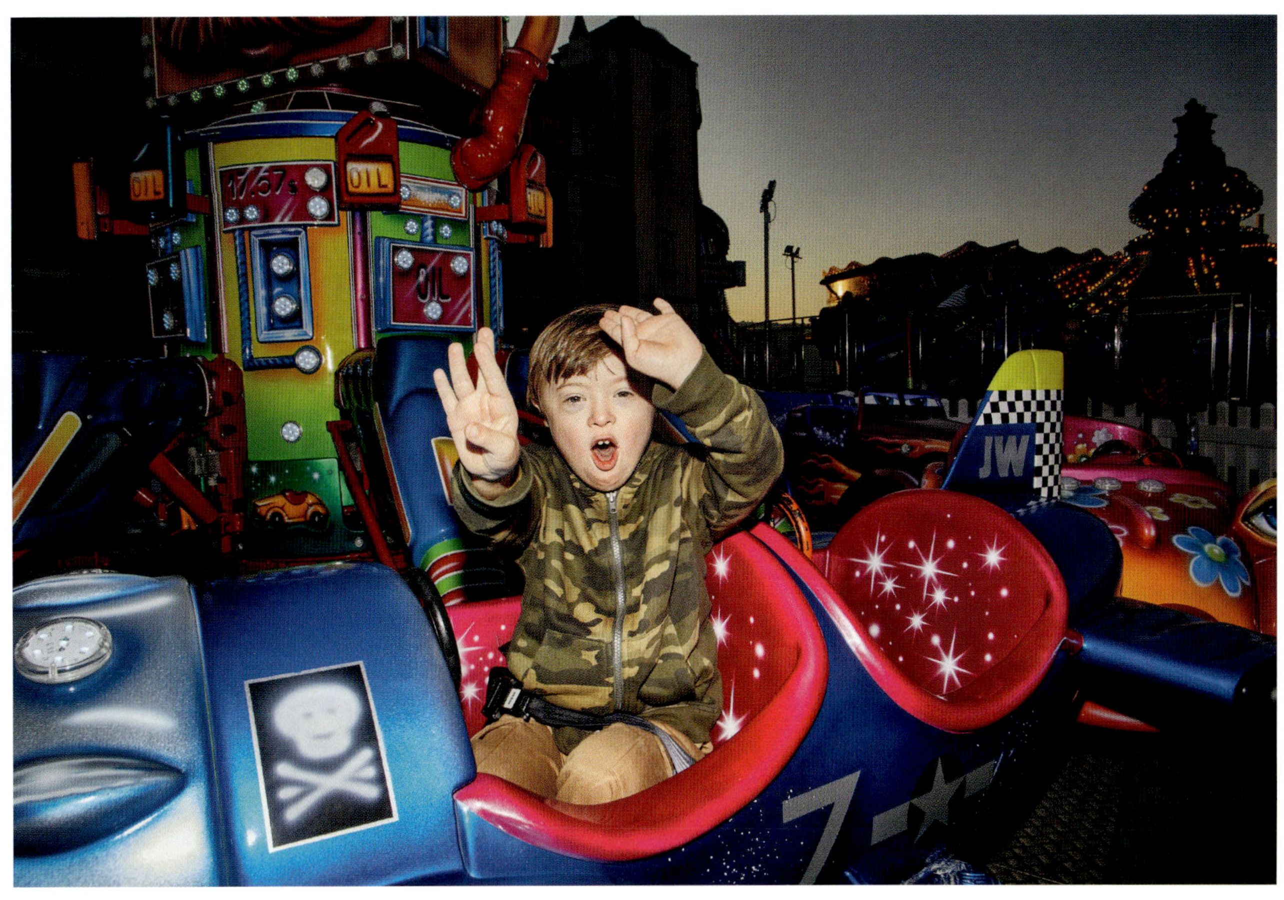

Soulla Petrou
Alex on Fairground Ride, 2024
From the series *Alex's Brighton Adventure*
Inkjet print

As the sun sets and the multicoloured, electric lights spark into life, Soulla Petrou captures this photograph on Brighton Palace Pier. Surrounded by the glossy, rainbow colours of the funfair is the photographer's eight-year-old nephew. Alex, who has Down's syndrome, brings a vivid energy to this portrait. Soella Petrou explains that her motivation was simply to 'record the joyous nature of life's little pleasures'. Born in Leeds to Greek Cypriot parents, Petrou began taking photographs when she received a Polaroid camera for her tenth birthday.

Ashley Bourne

Sir Michael Morpurgo, 2025
Inkjet print

This compelling portrait shows author Sir Michael
Morpurgo sat on his bed, notebook in hand, poised to
write. With a beret perched on his head and his socks
pulled up, Morpurgo's feet dangle just above the floor.
The author is known for his magical storytelling, exemplified
in works such as *War Horse* (1982). Bristol-based Ashley
Bourne has captured the vitality of the writer's mind and
work in the quirk and awkwardness of the pose and
composition. Commissioned to accompany an article
in the *Financial Times*, a central character in the image
is the single bed on which Morpurgo habitually writes
in his Devonshire home.

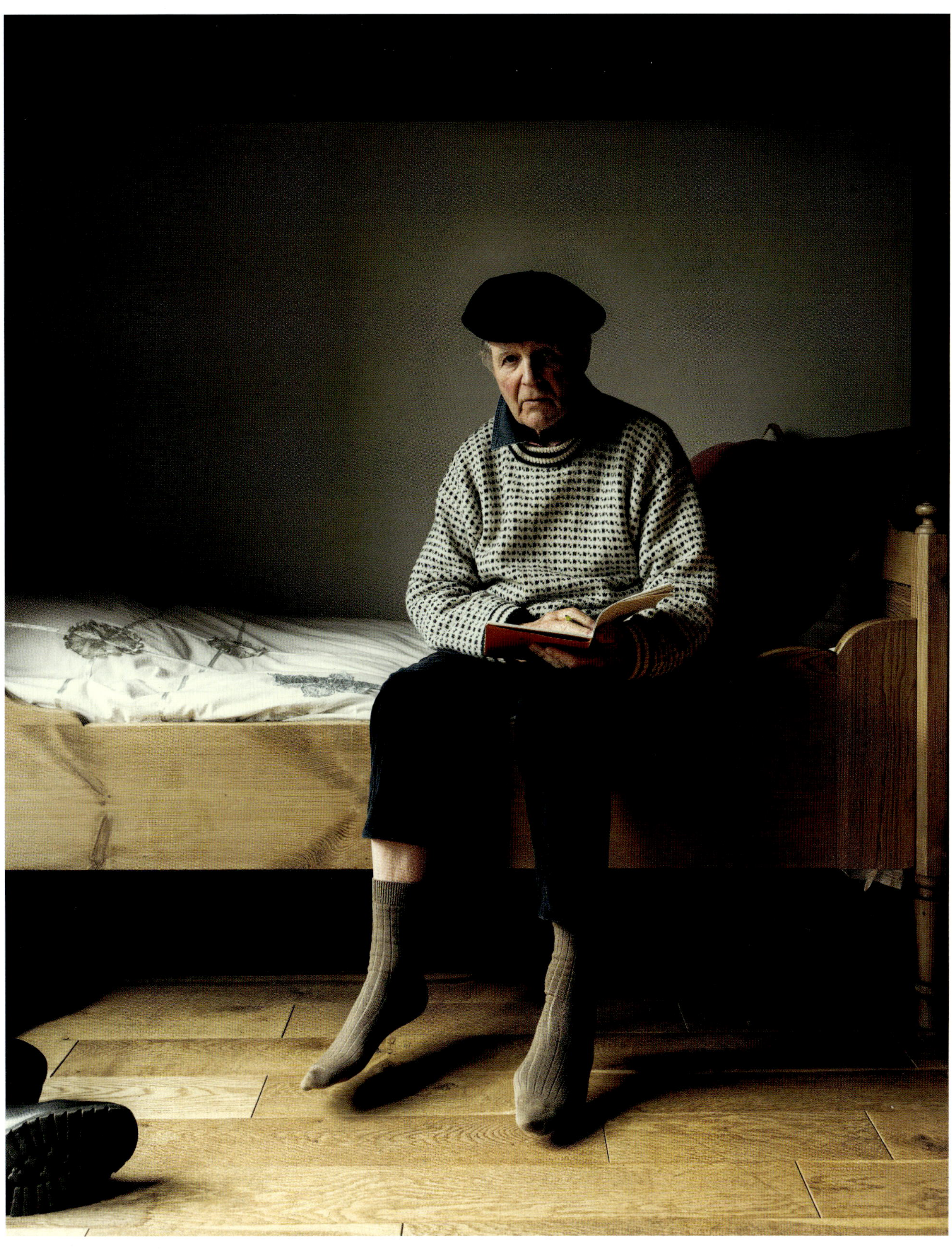

Elena Bianca Zagari

Ottavia sotto casa mia (Octavia outside my house), 2025
From the series *Un Mondo Proprio (A World Of One's Own)*
Chromogenic print

This portrait of Ottavia gives powerful expression to the sitter's personality, with her leopard print shirt, red hair, bold makeup and undaunted stare. Italian photographer Elena Bianca Zagari has been photographing Ottavia for several years, attracted to her sitter's intelligence, feminism and political activism. This photo, made in Naples, Italy, intends to confound the city's norms and expectations, challenging women's inferior position in its male dominated urban space and nightlife.

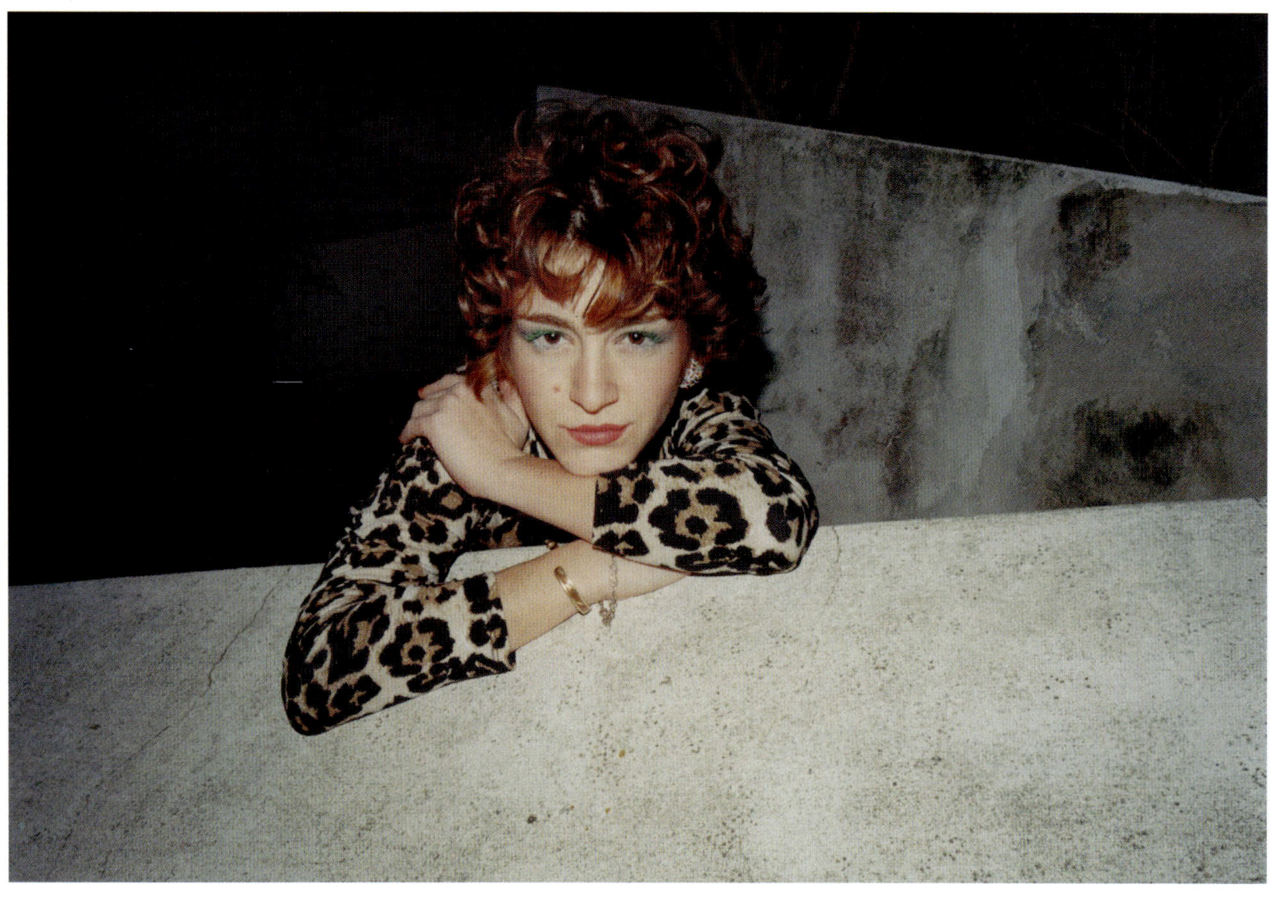

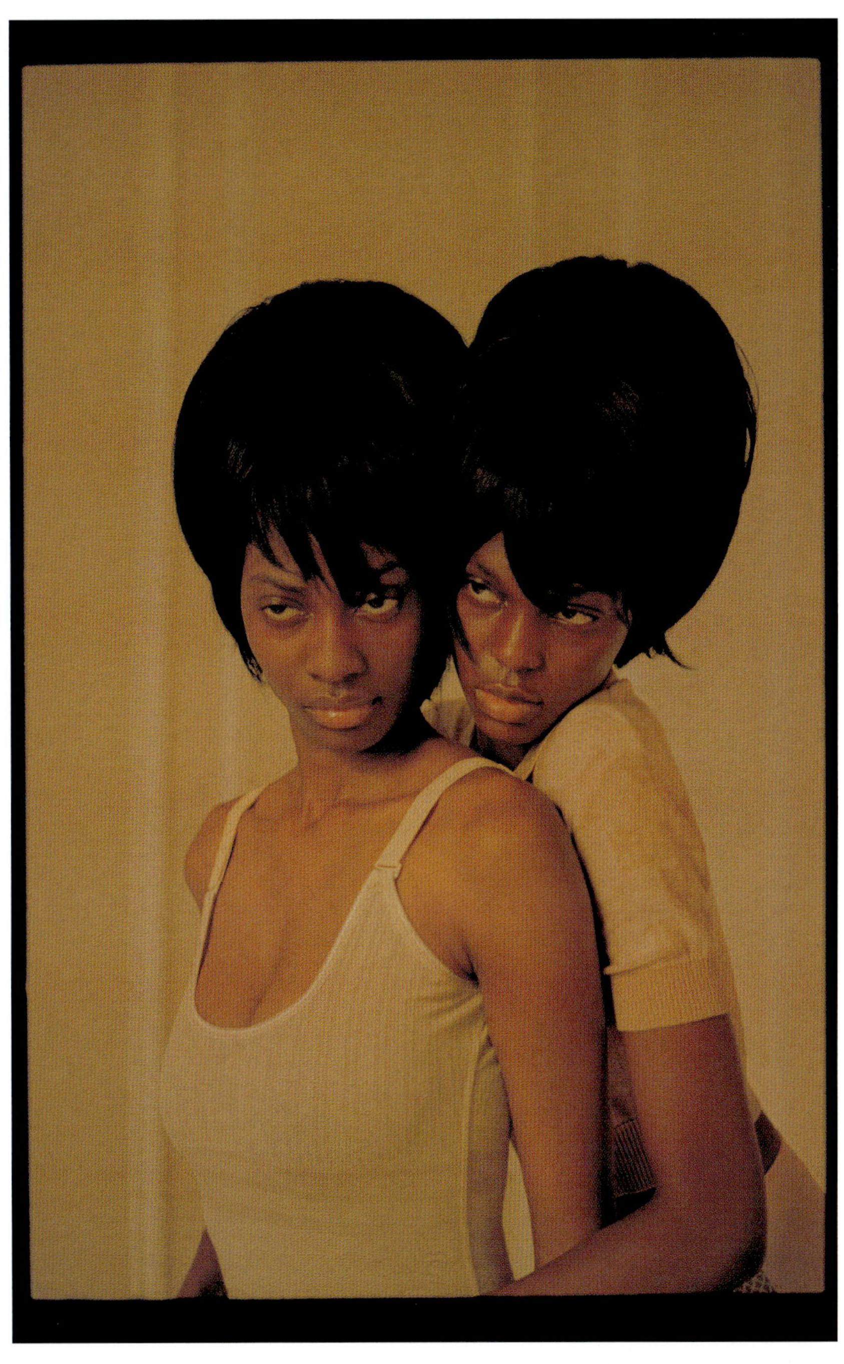

Dora Mois
Dream Girls, 2025
Inkjet print

With this portrait, the Romanian photographer Dora Mois evokes the style and spirit of the 1960s. A distinctive contemporary quality, however, can be seen in the formal abstractions, as in the conjoined beehive hairstyles of the two models. Mois explains her aim was 'to honour the beauty and power of Black women' while 'exploring intimacy, identity, and quiet rebellion – through softness, sisterhood and the strength found in following dreams before the world is watching'.

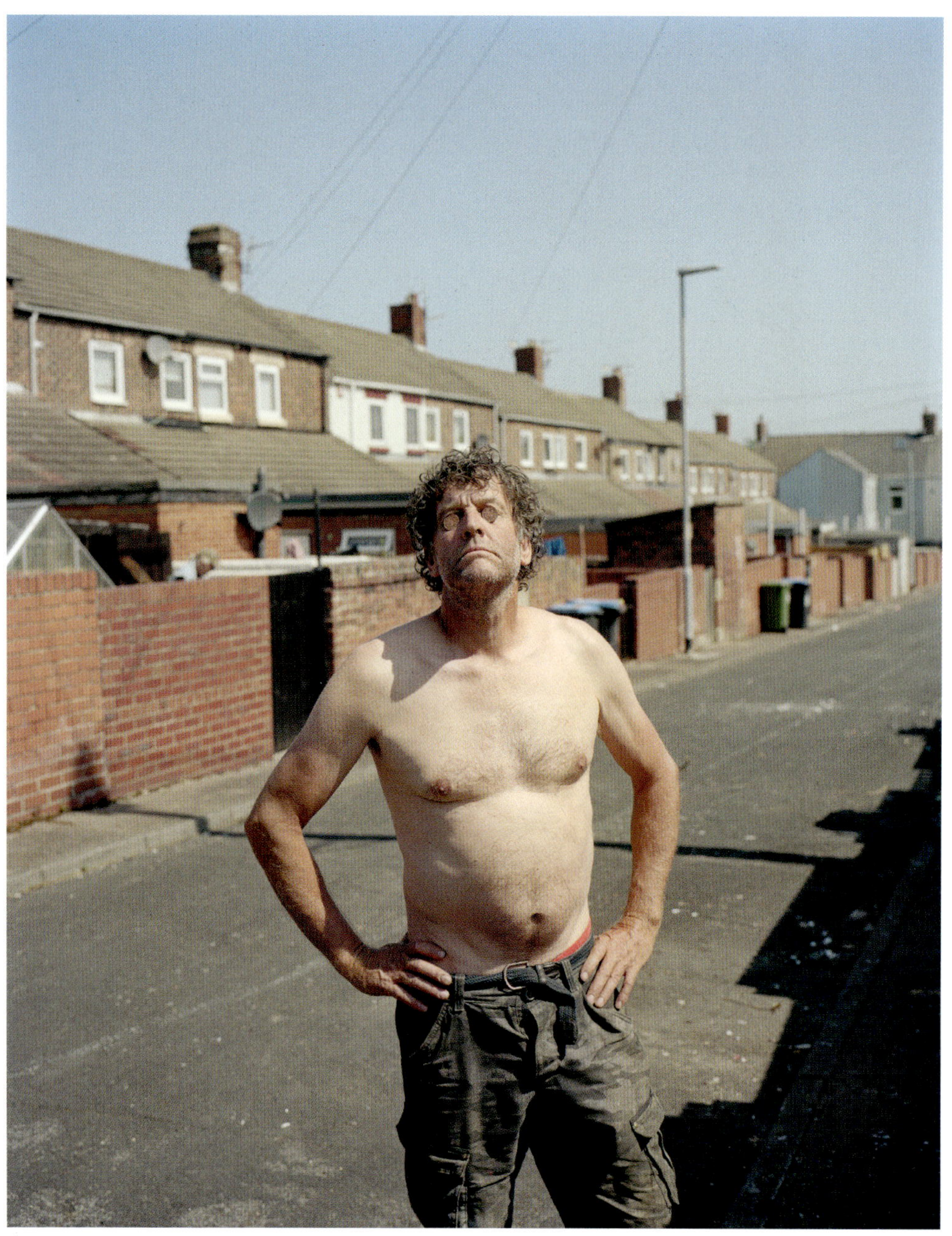

Ed Alcock

Pip, pennies and sunshine, 2024
Andrei, man of steel, 2024
From the series *Buried Treasure*
Chromogenic prints

For the series *Buried Treasure*, Ed Alcock follows his roots back to the mining village of Horden, County Durham, in order to 'explore the tales of my maternal family ... and the reality of a place that has become one of the poorest territories in Europe'. In these contrasting portraits of two Horden residents, the French-British photographer finds whimsical encounters in an unlikely setting. Pip, son and grandson of miners, poses in the sunshine with pennies on his eyes. Andrei, a Romanian who recently settled in the village, stands in the mist and bears a Superman t-shirt beneath his paint-splattered overalls.

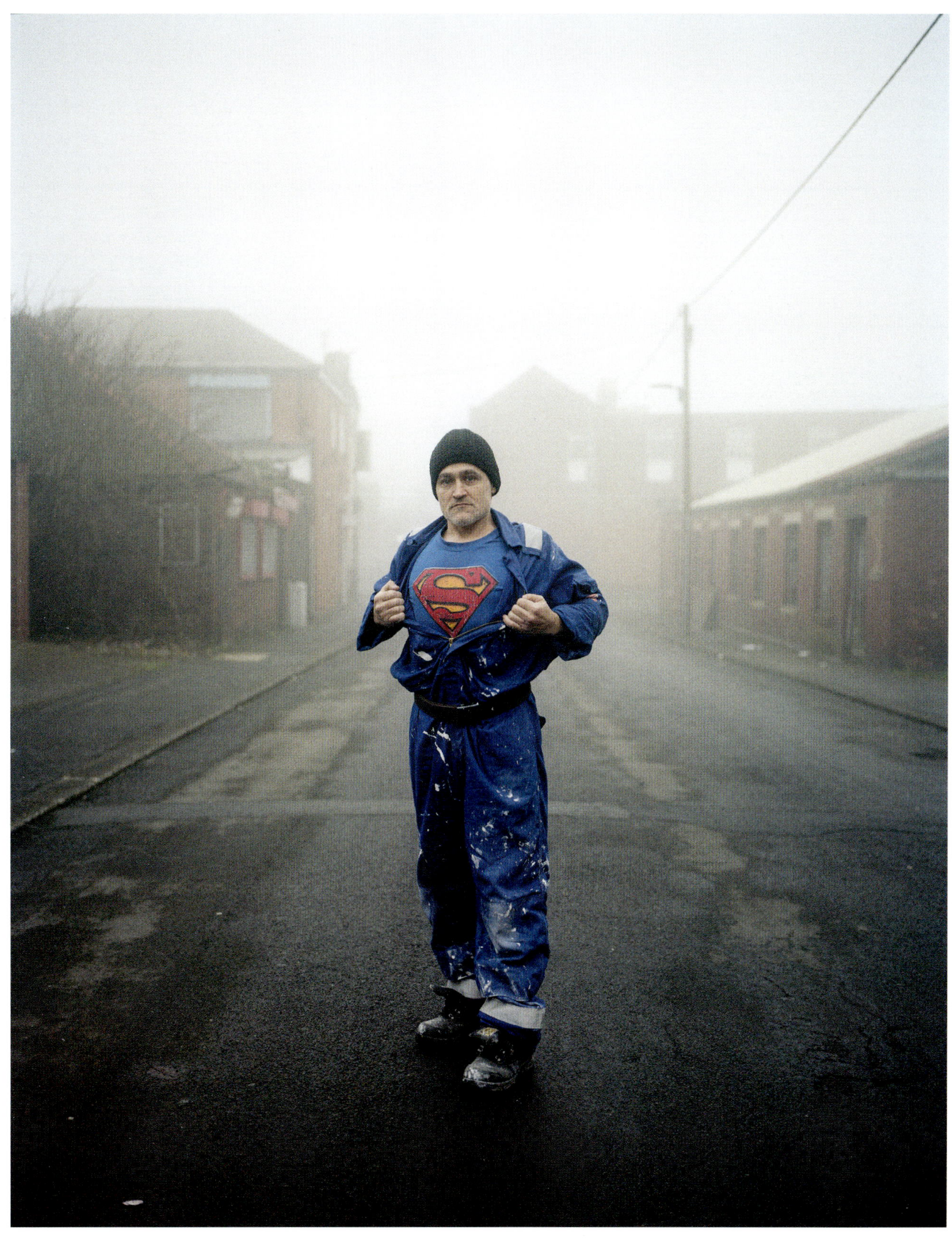

Jeremy Chih-Hao Chuang

24SPAP – Sweeping the floor, 2024
From the series *Ephemeral Intimacy*
Chromogenic print

Two men share a domestic space, yet they co-exist independently and do not interact. Jeremy Chih-Hao Chuang, a Taiwanese artist based in London, inserts himself as the fully clothed, seated figure to the left. This work is part of the ongoing series, *Ephemeral Intimacy*, in which Chuang photographs men he meets online, visiting their living spaces and capturing vulnerable moments to explore the subtle power dynamics that shape contemporary relationships. It was inspired by Chuang's personal experiences using dating apps where he was fascinated by the fleeting interactions and the emotionally lasting connections they produced.

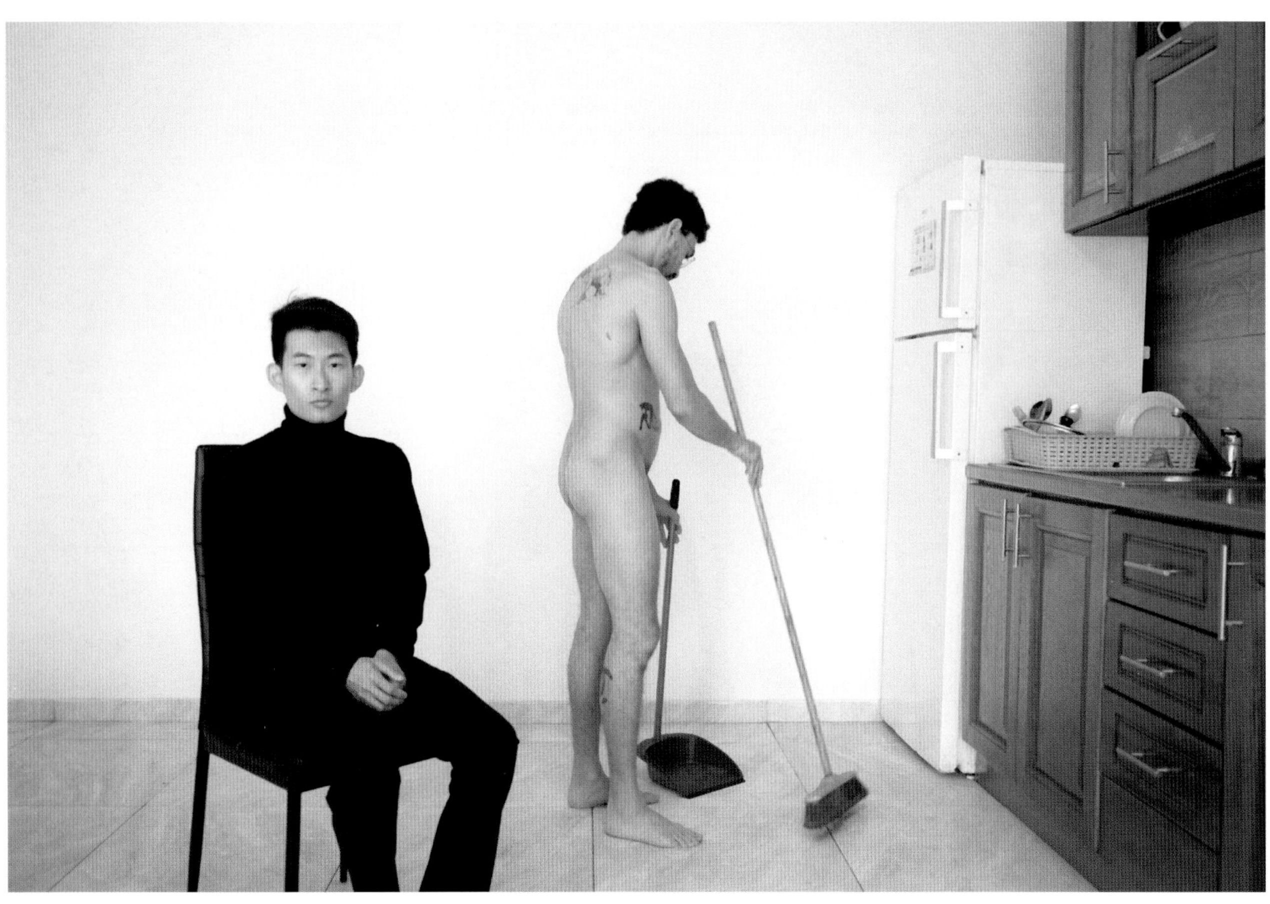

Jeremy Chih-Hao Chuang
24SPAP – Sweeping the floor, 2024
From the series *Ephemeral Intimacy*

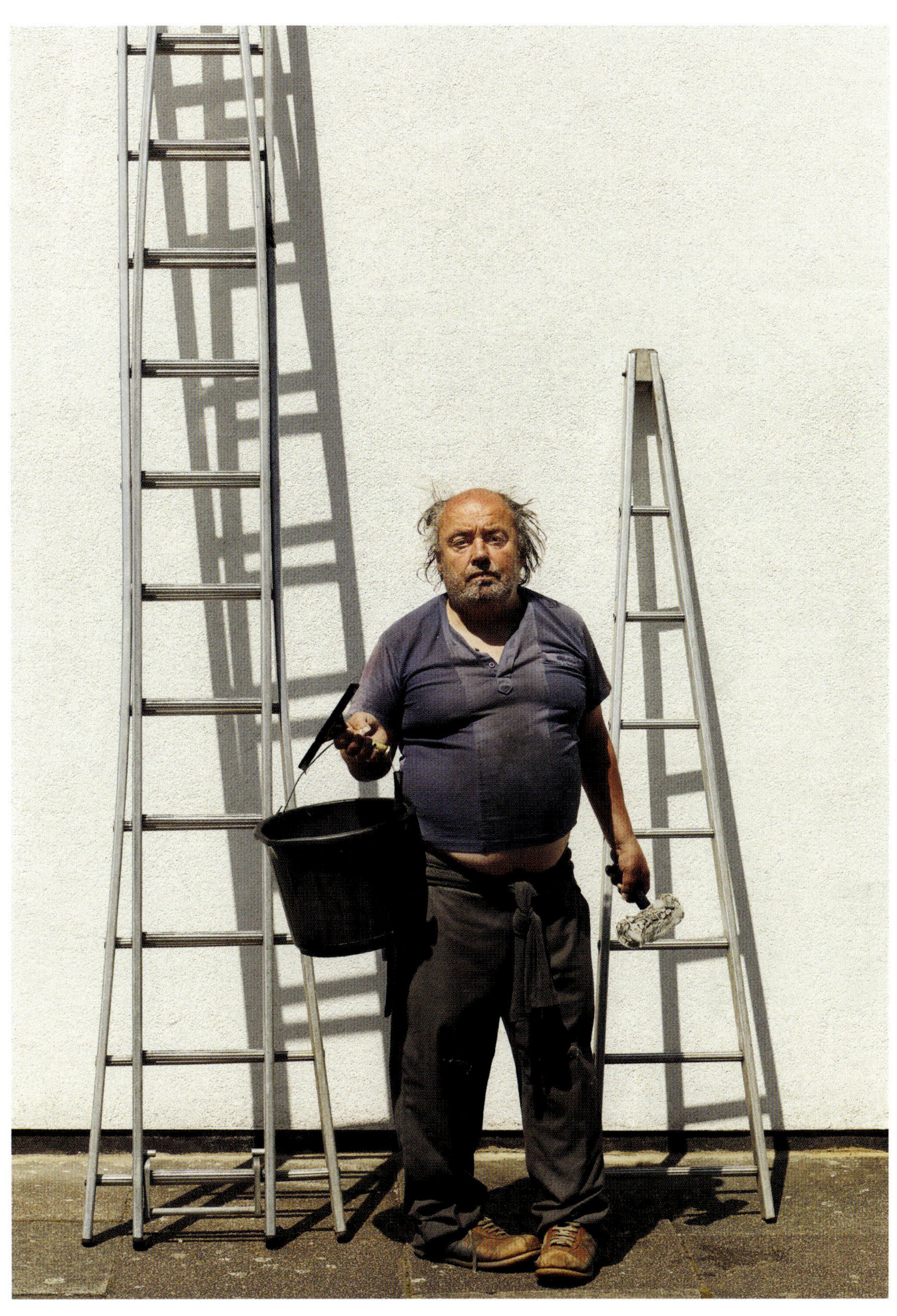

Debra Hurford Brown
Gary the Window Cleaner, 2024
Inkjet print

London-based Debra Hurford Brown is best known for her portraits of figures in the world of art and literature. Here, however, she photographs Gary, who has been cleaning her windows for 22 years. Contrasting the abstract, formal verticality of the ladders and shadows on the white wall with the singularity and humanity of the sitter, Hurford Brown constructs an absorbing image. The portrait conveys the character of its sitter, whose opinions are 'as strong as his tea'.

Rory Langdon-Down

Nyella, 2025
Nile, 2025
From the series *North London United*
Chromogenic prints

With Nyella's green and white-trimmed top echoing the tramlines and curtain behind her, this portrait evokes the colours of a football pitch. As Rory Langdon-Down explains, 'Nyella is at the heart of North London United, a football team founded by her father for young people with Down's syndrome'. The British photographer – whose great-great grandfather Dr John Langdon-Down discovered the condition – takes portraits of North London United's players, including five-year-old Nile, at the indoor pitch where they have trained since 2015. His joyful images attest to the team's motto, 'awareness is our currency'.

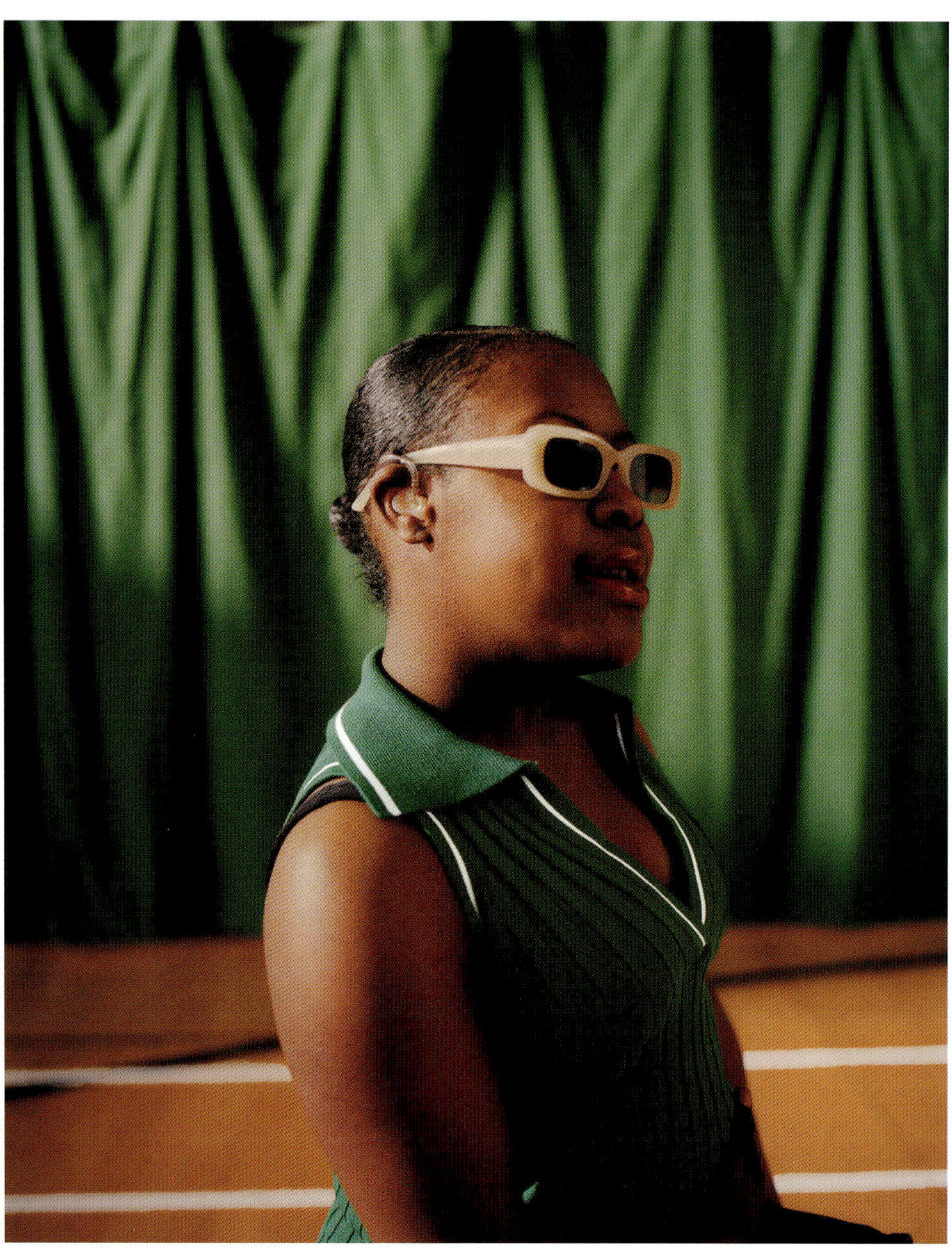

Rory Langdon-Down
Nyella, 2025
Nile, 2025
From the series *North London United*

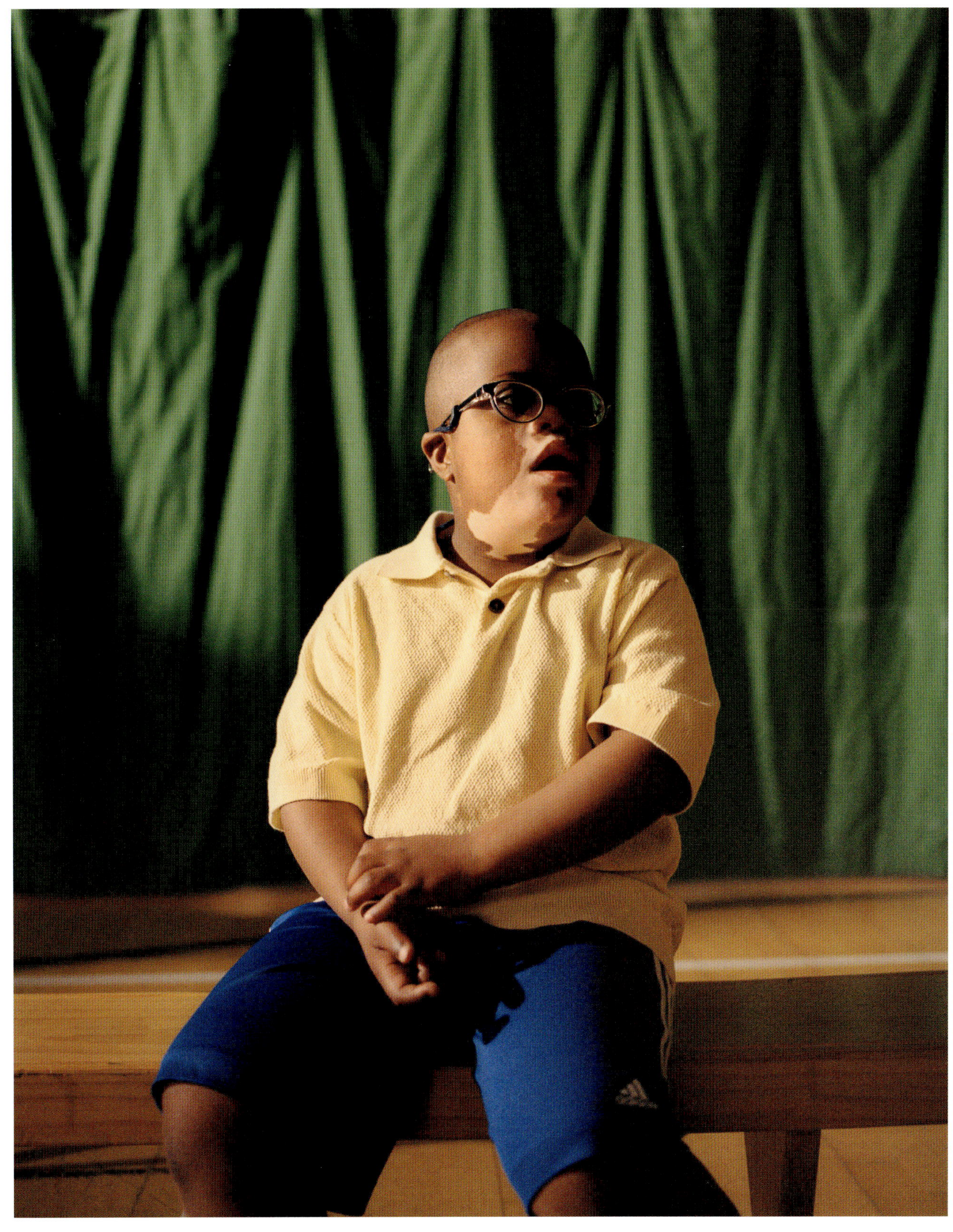

Ciril Jazbec

Leona 2, 2024
From the series *SILA: Between the Ice and Light*
Inkjet print

This striking portrait shows a young Inuit girl, Leona,
shortly after taking part in an ancient seal hunting ritual
deep in the Uummannaq Icefjord in northwest Greenland.
As Ciril Jazbec explains, 'For Leona, this moment was a
rare opportunity to witness and participate in a traditional
way of life, a way of life that may soon be lost to the
warming world.' Through long term documentary projects,
the Slovenian photographer seeks to raise awareness of
communities impacted by the climate crisis.

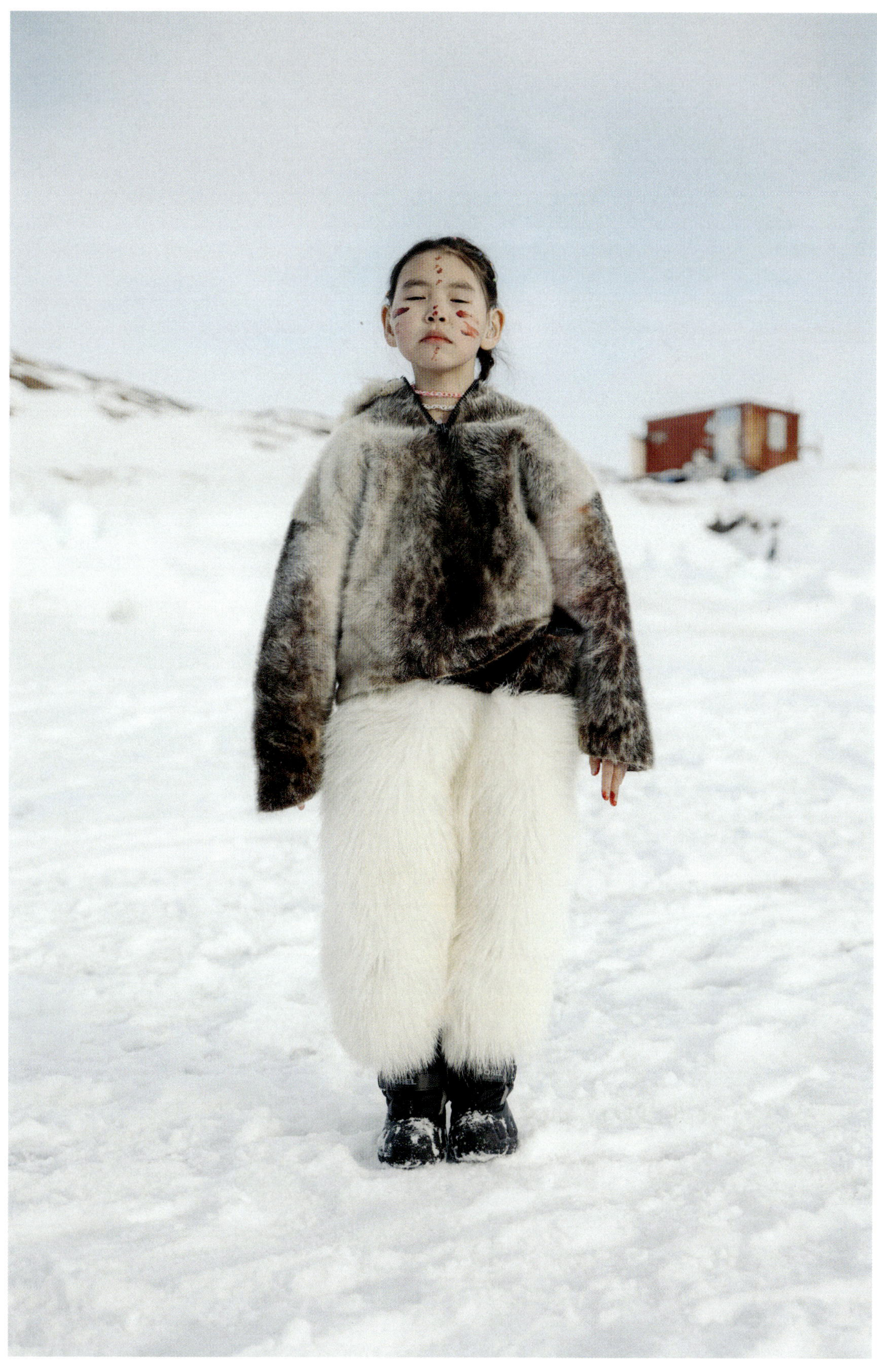

Published in Great Britain by
National Portrait Gallery Publications
National Portrait Gallery
St Martin's Place
London WC2H 0HE

Published to accompany the
Taylor Wessing Photo Portrait Prize 2025

Exhibited at the National Portrait Gallery, London
13 November 2025 to 8 February 2026

And the Millennium Gallery, Sheffield
21 February to 10 May 2026

Every purchase supports the National Portrait Gallery, London.

Information about the exhibition, competition and technical
information can be found at www.npg.org.uk/photoprize

Cover: *The Farmhand's Son* by William Sheepskin, 2024

Caption texts written by Clare Freestone, Curator, Photography,
Ruby Rees-Sheridan, Assistant Curator, Photography, Luke
Uglow, Assistant Curator and Nitasha Giran, Curatorial Assistant.

The capitalisation, spelling and punctuation of artwork titles is
presented as requested by the artist.

ISBN 978 1 85514 810 9

A catalogue record for this book is available from the
British Library.

The Director of the National Portrait Gallery would like to thank
the art handling team, Stuart Ager, Poppy Andrews, Rachael
Bailey, Katherine Biggs, Zoe Bott, Sam Brown, Sophie Colley,
Jessica Daley, Rachel Dunlop, Andrea Easey, Clare Freestone,
Flavia Frigeri, Nitasha Giran, Kara Green, Jahnavi Inniss,
Claire Irvine, Jemma Jacobs, Chloe Jamieson, Priti Kothary,
Emmanuelle Largeteau, Francesca Laws, Thulani Maseko,
Tanya Millard, Abi Ponton, Skye Redman, Charlotte Regan,
Amber Sherlock, Jude Simmons, Georgia Smith, Liz Smith,
Anna Starling, Eloise Stewart, Anna Sorrell, Benjamin Townsend,
Oliver Tratt, Luke Uglow, Denise Vogelsang, Rachel Whitehouse,
Helen Whiteoak, Rosie Wilson and especially Clementine
Williamson, Exhibitions Manager, Callum Brunton, Exhibitions
Assistant, Ruby Rees-Sheridan, Assistant Curator, Photography
and Sabina Jaskot-Gill, Senior Curator, Photography, for their
hard work on the project.

Director of Commercial and Operations:
Anna Starling
Publisher:
Kara Green
Production Manager:
Priti Kothary
Project Editor:
Jemma Jacobs
Design:
Peter Dawson, www.gradedesign.com

Origination by Altaimage London

Printed and bound in the UK by Park Communications

This publication is printed on FSC certified paper and has
been manufactured using 100% vegetable oil-based inks and
100% offshore wind electricity sourced from UK wind. Park
Communications Ltd is a carbon neutral production company.

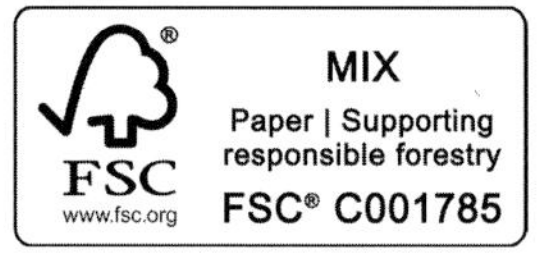